EXPLORING TEACHER EDUCATOR KNOWLEDGE

ADVANCES IN RESEARCH ON TEACHING

Series Editor: Cheryl J. Craig

Co-Series Editor: Stefinee Pinnegar

Recent Volumes:

Volume 19:	From Teacher Thinking to Teachers and Teaching: The Evolution of a Research Community
Volume 20:	Innovations in Science Teacher Education in the Asia Pacific
Volume 21:	Research on Preparing Preservice Teachers to Work Effectively With Emergent Bilinguals
Volume 22:	International Teacher Education: Promising Pedagogies (Part A)
Volume 22:	International Teacher Education: Promising Pedagogies (Part B)
Volume 23:	Narrative Conceptions of Knowledge: Towards Understanding Teacher Attrition
Volume 24:	Research on Preparing Inservice Teachers to Work Effectively With Emergent Bilinguals
Volume 25:	Exploring Pedagogies for Diverse Learners Online
Volume 26:	Knowing, Becoming, Doing as Teacher Educators: Identity, Intimate Scholarship, Inquiry
Volume 27:	Innovations in English Language Arts Teacher Education
Volume 28:	Crossroads of the Classroom: Narrative Intersections of Teacher Knowledge and Subject Matter
Volume 29:	Culturally Sustaining and Revitalizing Pedagogies
Volume 30:	Self-Study of Language and Literacy Teacher Education Practices
Volume 31:	Decentering the Researcher in Intimate Scholarship: Critical Posthuman Methodological Perspectives in Education
Volume 32:	Essays on Teaching Education and the Inner Drama of Teaching: Where Biography and History Meet
Volume 33:	Landscapes, Edges, and Identity-Making

Volume 34:	Exploring Self Toward Expanding Teaching, Teacher Education and Practitioner Research
Volume 35:	Preparing Teachers to Teach the STEM Disciplines in America's Urban Schools
Volume 36:	Luminous Literacies: Localized Teaching and Teacher Education
Volume 37:	Developing Knowledge Communities Through Partnerships for Literacy
Volume 38:	Understanding Excessive Teacher and Faculty Entitlement: Digging at the Roots
Volume 39:	Global Meaning Making: Disrupting and Interrogating International Language and Literacy Research and Teaching
Volume 40:	Making Meaning With Readers and Texts: Beginning Teachers' Meaning-Making From Classroom Events
Volume 41:	Teacher Education in the Wake of Covid-19: ISATT 40th Anniversary Yearbook
Volume 42:	Teaching and Teacher Education in International Contexts: ISATT 40th Anniversary Yearbook
Volume 43:	Approaches to Teaching and Teacher Education: ISATT 40th Anniversary Yearbook
Volume 44:	Studying Teaching and Teacher Education: ISATT 40th Anniversary Yearbook
Volume 45:	Drawn to the Flame: Teachers' Stories of Burnout
Volume 46:	Smudging Composition Lines of Identity and Teacher Knowledge: Cross-Cultural Narrative Inquiries Into Teaching and Learning
Volume 47:	After Excessive Teacher and Faculty Entitlement: Expanding the Space for Healing and Human Flourishing Through Ideological Becoming

ADVANCES IN RESEARCH ON TEACHING   VOLUME 48

EXPLORING TEACHER EDUCATOR KNOWLEDGE

BY

CELINA DULUDE LAY
Brigham Young University, USA

United Kingdom – North America – Japan
India – Malaysia – China

Emerald Publishing Limited
Emerald Publishing, Floor 5, Northspring, 21-23 Wellington Street, Leeds LS1 4DL

First edition 2025

Copyright ©2025 Celina Dulude Lay.
Published under exclusive licence by Emerald Publishing Limited.

Reprints and permissions service
Contact: www.copyright.com

No part of this book may be reproduced, stored in a retrieval system, transmitted in any form or by any means electronic, mechanical, photocopying, recording or otherwise without either the prior written permission of the publisher or a licence permitting restricted copying issued in the UK by The Copyright Licensing Agency and in the USA by The Copyright Clearance Center. Any opinions expressed in the chapters are those of the authors. Whilst Emerald makes every effort to ensure the quality and accuracy of its content, Emerald makes no representation implied or otherwise, as to the chapters' suitability and application and disclaims any warranties, express or implied, to their use.

British Library Cataloguing in Publication Data
A catalogue record for this book is available from the British Library

ISBN: 978-1-83549-883-5 (Print)
ISBN: 978-1-83549-882-8 (Online)
ISBN: 978-1-83549-884-2 (Epub)

ISSN: 1479-3687 (Series)

Printed and bound by CPI Group (UK) Ltd, Croydon, CR0 4YY

INVESTOR IN PEOPLE

CONTENTS

About the Author   *ix*

Foreword to A Self-Study of the Shifts in Teacher Educator Knowledge Resulting From the Move From In-Person to Online Instruction   *xi*

How Can We Frame an Inquiry Into Teacher Educator Knowledge?   *1*

What Do We Know About Teacher Education, and How Do We Use That Knowledge?   *13*

What Methodology and Accompanying Strategies Allow Us to Uncover Teacher Educator Knowledge?   *35*

How Can Analytic Narrative Vignettes Allow Complex Representation of Data?   *51*

What Does the Planning Vignette Reveal About Teacher Educator Knowledge?   *63*

What Does the Teaching Vignette Reveal About Teacher Educator Knowledge?   *77*

What Does the Reflecting Vignette Reveal About Teacher Educator Knowledge?   *91*

What Are the Strands of Teacher Educator Knowledge Embedded Across the Vignettes?   *103*

What Does This Study Contribute to Our Understanding About Teacher Education? *113*

What Are the Implications of Studies of Teacher Educator Knowledge for Teacher Education? *123*

References *129*

ABOUT THE AUTHOR

Dr Celina Dulude Lay is an Adjunct Professor and a Teacher Educator at Brigham Young University in Provo, Utah. She holds a Master's degree from the University of Utah, with a focus on curriculum design and teaching reading. She earned her doctorate in 2021 from Brigham Young University. Dr Lay has been engaged in the study of her own practice since she was an undergraduate, writing a thesis on the development of teacher identity during student teaching. She has taught secondary English Language Arts and French and enjoyed the energy of teaching adolescents. Currently, she enjoys the energy of her own children, as well as the teacher candidates she teaches in courses on adolescent development and classroom management. For more than a decade, she has also designed and taught university courses in TESOL K-12 for supporting the language and literacy development of English learners. Dr Lay is committed to supporting teacher candidates in their preparation and improving her own practice.

FOREWORD TO *A SELF-STUDY OF THE SHIFTS IN TEACHER EDUCATOR KNOWLEDGE RESULTING FROM THE MOVE FROM IN-PERSON TO ONLINE INSTRUCTION*

Contributed by Eline Vanassche

About 15 years ago, I took my first steps as a junior researcher at an educational conference in the Netherlands. It was a memorable experience for multiple reasons, not all of which deserve space in the preface of this book. I presented a systematic literature review of the Self-Study of Teacher Education Practices (S-STEP) approach, which was largely unknown in European teacher education practice and research at the time. The literature review was framed as part of a dissertation aimed at understanding the nature of the knowledge, identities and understandings invested in the work of educating teachers.

My initiation into academia was met with some critical questions, two of which remain vivid in memory to this day and are also relevant to understanding the contribution of the book at hand. These questions went something along the lines of: What makes teacher educators so unique that you would dedicate a dissertation to this professional group? And why do you consider professional development as a form of research? Admittedly, these questions have become stronger in my mind than they were perhaps intended or formulated 15 years ago. At the time, as a junior researcher, I struggled to respond. I had prepared for questions about the methodology and practical implications of my research, but my notes did not prepare me to address fundamental criticisms of my dissertation's core premises. In hindsight, however, these questions should hardly have come as a surprise. They reflected the then prevailing view that teacher educators simply teach their subject in higher education. While it was not considered entirely irrelevant that their students are students of teaching (of a particular subject), strong subject knowledge was considered the foundation for the work of educating teachers. The S-STEP community and research was met with suspicion from the more dominant post-positivist research approaches at best or considered yet another exemplar of the perceived lack of rigor in teacher education research at worst.

Over the years, I have matured and learned to address such questions, just as the field of teacher educator and S-STEP research has matured and developed. The unique complexity of the work of educating teachers is now better understood and appreciated. I also believe that "we," as S-STEP researchers, have perfected "our" practice and learned how to better speak the language of researchers and policymakers while staying true to our own critical agenda (see also Vanassche & Berry, 2020). That said, much work remains to be done as the significance of S-STEP research in and for teacher education is often still judged by the strength of its latest achievement. Each study bears to some degree the burden of demonstrating the worth and value of the community at large. This might seem like a pessimistic view, especially in the preface of a book reporting on a self-study of practice, yet it also signals an important opportunity. Persistent critique keeps us vigilant and proactive in showcasing the transformative potential of our work, advocating for its recognition and integration into more mainstream educational research (a tenuous term in itself).

This book is a strong testimony to that ongoing journey of legitimizing and advancing S-STEP. It demonstrates clear understanding of the types of knowledge claims that resonate with a wider audience while honoring and keeping intact the complexity of the work of educating teachers. In the opening chapter, it is stated that "this study focused on the particular" (p. 4), in line with the S-STEP approach. I would add that this study succeeds in capturing the general in the particular. It shows the potential of research that starts from personal practice, experiences, challenges, and ponderings to also achieve relevance that extends well beyond the local context in which the research was carried out through careful consideration of methods and theory.

The self-study research presented in this book begins with the unexpected and rapid transition from in-person to online teaching in the spring of 2020 due to COVID-19. The transition was initially described as emergency remote teaching in a time of crisis (e.g., Bozkurt & Sharma, 2020), suggesting a degree of forgiveness regarding the inexperience of teacher educators and the challenges associated with inadequate online infrastructure. Gradually, however, it evolved into more stable remote or blended teaching contexts, now commonplace or even mandated across many institutions globally, with associated expectations that such approaches are as effective, or even more effective, than in-person teaching. What constitutes effectiveness is often vaguely defined or confused with cost-effectiveness from the program's perspective or time-effectiveness from the students' perspective. This highlights the marked need for research that focuses on the meaning and reconfiguration of practice in online formats in the post-pandemic teacher education landscape.

This book fills this gap in crucial ways. The self-study work presented here authentically opens up the dilemmas of online teaching and planning. In so doing, it also shows the capacity of large transitions to uncover and rework our tacit and embodied understandings of what it means to teach about teaching. Careful analysis of the data gathered in the process of planning, teaching, and reflecting on an online course together with a critical friend contributed seven strands of teacher educator knowledge that resonate well beyond online practice as a teacher educator. The strands unpacked and brought to life in the book are: Content Knowledge, Fixed and Fluid Elements, Knowledge of Milieu, Pedagogical Intent, Preservice Teacher Knowledge and Belief, Value and Fragility of Relationships, and Theory Matters. These strands of knowledge serve to underscore the complexity of teacher education practice and caution that the shift to online teaching is not merely a transfer in methods or modalities. Celina Dulude Lay's work clearly demonstrates that the question of the effectiveness of online teaching, much like in-person teaching, cannot be answered without serious consideration of its intended goals and outcomes, including questions about the types of teachers we aim to educate and why we deem this important. This is a crucial missing voice in the field of research on online teaching and teacher education.

This book shows the capacity of self-study research to capture and hold onto the ambivalence and contradictions of teacher education and teacher educator knowledge. Findings are presented in the form of three analytic vignettes, with each vignette containing "representative exemplars of events, conversations, and ongoing analysis" (p. 39) that occurred during the phases of planning for the course, teaching the course, and reflecting on the course. By delving into concrete and real-life scenarios, they illuminate the often-overlooked subtleties and contextualities that influence our decisions in and for practice and our reflections on the meaning and value of these decisions. The vignettes not only provide an exceptional window into the experiences of online teaching but also offer an interesting framework for imagining new and different possibilities for practice, both for the self-study researcher involved and for the larger audience engaging with these vignettes.

The book illustrates what professional learning and development as a teacher educator looks like, emphasizing the development of scholarship rather than the development and accumulation of knowledge. The author demonstrates scholarship by making explicit and developing ways to deal with the complexities, uncertainties, and nuances of online teacher education, and by sharing these in a meaningful manner with others. The value of this self-study research lies in the commitment of this teacher educator to provide insights into how the evolving understandings and strands of knowledge revealed in the process of planning, teaching, and reflecting on an online course for student teachers became part of, informed, and influenced her practice. This allows others to build upon these strands of knowledge as a lens to examine their own practice and development.

It serves as a prime example of what Cochran-Smith and Lytle (2004) described as "working the dialectic." By working the dialectic of researching and teaching about teaching, Celina Lay blends theory and practice, knowledge and action, inquiry and experience, and transforms a private account of practice into a scholarly and public contribution that invites critical reflection and review from the community. Chapter by chapter, she uncovers the enormous potential of giving up the distinction between being a teacher educator and being a researcher. She carefully navigates the pitfalls of individualism and navel-gazing (Kelchtermans & Hamilton, 2004; Vanassche & Kelchtermans, 2015) by avoiding overemphasizing idiosyncratic challenges, questions, and accounts of practice, which, while offering opportunities for professional development, may hold little relevance to the broader teaching and learning community, while also sidestepping the trap of generalizability, which, though suitable for traditional research paradigms, often lacks practical relevance.

This self-study is much more than a strong piece of research; it serves as a beacon illuminating the tacit and embodied dimensions of being and continuously becoming a teacher educator. It shows the deep professional reward and commitment that can stem from honoring and staying true to the complexity of the work of educating teachers. The way it is reported allows it to perform this transformative potential for its readers as well. The book is a tribute to S-STEP and the at times frustrating yet also rewording and nurturing complexity and messiness of the work of educating teachers.

As with anything in life, firsthand experience carries greater power than incomplete attempts by others to convey the meaning or significance of what you are about to experience. Consider this an invitation to embark on and engage with this work.

REFERENCES

Bozkurt, A., & Sharma, R. C. (2020). Emergency remote teaching in a time of global crisis due to Coronavirus pandemic. *Asian Journal of Distance Education*, *15*(1), 1–6.

Cochran-Smith, M., & Lytle, S. L. (2004). Practitioner inquiry, knowledge, and university culture. In J. J. Loughran, M. L. Hamilton, V. K. LaBoskey, & T. Russell (Eds.), *International handbook of self-study of teaching and teacher education practices* (pp. 601–649). Springer.

Kelchtermans, G., & Hamilton, M. L. (2004). The dialects of passion and theory: Exploring the relation between self-study and emotion. In J. Loughran, M. L. Hamilton, V. K. LaBoskey, & T. Russell (Eds.), *International handbook of self-study of teaching and teacher education practices* (pp. 785–810). Kluwer Academic.

Vanassche, E., & Berry, A. (2020). Teacher educator knowledge, practice, and S-STTEP research. In J. Kitchen, A. Berry, S. M. Bullock, A. R. Crowe, M. Taylor, H. Guðjónsdóttir, & L. Thomas (Eds.), *International handbook of self-study of teaching and teacher education practices* (2nd ed., pp. 177–214). Springer.

Vanassche, E., & Kelchtermans, G. (2015). The state of the art in self-study of teacher education practices: A systematic literature review. *Journal of Curriculum Studies*, *47*(4), 508–528. http://dx.doi.org/10.1080/00220272.2014.995712

HOW CAN WE FRAME AN INQUIRY INTO TEACHER EDUCATOR KNOWLEDGE?

ABSTRACT

Given the competing contexts of teacher education (universities, school placements, online programs, diversity placements, etc.), it is important to uncover what teacher educator knowledge concerning curriculum development emerges in design, implementation, and instruction. The intimate and particular nature of self-study of teacher education practice as a method of inquiry was chosen for its potential ability to add to what we know about teacher educators themselves. In particular, during the transition from in-person to online teaching contexts, teacher educator knowledge is potentially revealed. Because transitions are an important time to uncover tacit and embodied understanding, this self-study of teacher education practice (S-STEP) was framed as an inquiry into what teacher educator knowledge is carried forward or changed during a time of shifting teaching context such as creating and enacting online teaching, developing a course, program evaluation, etc. To understand the puzzle guiding this research and the framework developed for study, the chapters of the book are then briefly outlined.

Keywords: Self-study of practice; preservice teacher education; online education; teacher educator knowledge; curriculum design; teacher educator; teacher knowledge; tacit knowledge

"What does your mom do?"

My 10-year-old son enjoys answering this question, "She is a teacher who teaches teachers how to teach." It sounds like an Edward Lear nonsense poem. As a teacher educator, yes, I am a former teacher who now prepares teachers. But I am still in essence a teacher (Pinnegar et al., 2018). I do recognize, however, that across time, my knowledge as a teacher educator developed out of and alongside my identity and knowledge as teacher. I could begin tracing my teaching knowledge with my earliest memories of helping my dad in his classroom and as the oldest of four, helping with the family after school while my mom went back to school for a teaching license. I could also reflect on teaching experiences as one

---

Exploring Teacher Educator Knowledge
Advances in Research on Teaching, Volume 48, 1–12
Copyright © 2025 Celina Dulude Lay
Published under exclusive licence by Emerald Publishing Limited
ISSN: 1479-3687/doi:10.1108/S1479-368720240000048001

of the oldest cousins, as a babysitter, as a volunteer with many youth programs, camp counselor, dance instructor, piano teacher, and so on. Still, I would say my formal knowledge and understanding of teaching as a profession began when I chose English Teaching as a major at Brigham Young University in 1993.

At that time, I made a conscious choice to have the word "Teaching" follow behind the word English in my major and the French in my minor. Perhaps, as a child of educators, teaching was a vocation I understood, and part of the reason I chose teaching was because I did not know what other possibilities there were for me. But I think it wasn't just that. Another distinct memory I have at that time is that teaching felt like a calling. I loved studying literature and learning how to write better. At the same time, I recognized that I was equally intrigued with the puzzle of how to engage young minds in reading and writing and language.

Especially relevant to my current teacher educator knowledge is learning gained during student teaching and my first-year teaching experiences. When I student taught, my mentor teacher had recently been awarded Teacher of the Year by her school district. This district currently employs more than 3,000 teachers. I was fortunate to be in the classroom of a master teacher who engaged middle school students, both gifted and struggling, with masterful pedagogy and curriculum crafted to meet diverse needs. Honestly, those months were like drinking from a fire hose and as a novice; there was no way for me to take it all in. I continued learning from those months of student teaching in the years that followed, when I had my wits more about me and could better reflect upon the reasons behind choices and moves she had made, such as in informal assessments, the planning of a semester or year or unit, and other nuances of classroom curriculum, organization, and management.

My first year of teaching was especially relevant to gaining knowledge as a teacher, and later as a teacher educator, because of the context. I accepted a position in a residential behavioral treatment school, where inner-city children were sent from school districts in LA and Chicago and where the children of upper-class families were part of my teaching responsibility. During this time, I began a master's degree in education, and this led to a deepening of my theoretical and practical knowledge. For example, at the university, I was learning cognitive strategies for teaching difficult concepts. After class, later into the night, I would try out one of those strategies with the students in my classes in mind, connecting what I was learning in graduate studies to the needs of real students and real lesson plans. By creating an activity for my students, I was naturally following a cycle of reflection and strengthening my connections of theory and practice. All of my students had things on their minds, trauma and struggles of all kinds, so when they sat in my class, it felt like a quiet victory when I could trigger curiosity or see them engage with an idea or discussion. Other university courses taught me more about multicultural education, and as I tested various theoretical lenses, I examined my own biases and sought for ways to influence class culture and connect learning in meaningful ways to my diverse students.

After teaching at the private residential school, I took a job teaching in a public junior high school. The things I learned from experience and the things I learned from study coalesced and formed a strong base for informing my future teacher educator knowledge as I often even as a teacher considered what pre-service teachers need to experience to have richer identities as teachers and be better positioned to build on the knowledge they already have. Recently, my co-teacher at the junior high, who I had lost track of after so many years, knocked on my door to invite signatures for a state school board member she was supporting. Back then, we taught eighth grade English together for struggling readers and were able to give extra support and creative energy to the students with individualized learning plans, as well as those who felt despondent about their reading skills. Ever since then I had drawn on what I learned about adolescent reading strategies and what I learned teaching with her, my teacher educator knowledge firmly rooted in this mentoring relationship and teaching context. I was so glad to see her on my porch. It did not surprise me to hear that she also teaches at a university and serves on the state school board. Teacher knowledge is often compelled to be put to use.

After that year teaching eighth grade English, I took a rest from my teaching labors with a difficult pregnancy and to be home with my long-awaited child. Seven years later, I had another baby, this time a boy, followed by three more. My teaching knowledge gained in classrooms and in university courses did not lie dormant during this stage. I recognize that my years as a mother developing learning opportunities for my children incorporated knowledge from all these sources (see Pinnegar et al., 2005, 2018).

As I took up the teaching of university courses, increased my involvement in the development of curriculum, and conducted research on my practice, my teacher educator knowledge and teacher knowledge became intricately entangled. Engaging in research on developing my practices as a teacher educator was particularly impacted through my work in developing courses for practicing and preservice teachers learning to work with English as a Second Language (ESL) students in regular classroom instruction, both elementary and secondary. This work emerged as I was studying for a doctorate in teacher education and developing courses for preservice teachers during COVID-19.

In one sense, that is a lot of baggage. I have had exposure to a variety of useful theoretical frameworks and experience teaching in a private school setting, public secondary schools, in my home, and higher education. There are other interesting experiences I could list as well that are unique to me and have shaped my teaching expertise and skill. The point is that each teacher educator comes to the classroom (because we came *from* the classroom either as students or teachers or both) having walked a particular path of schooling and teaching that has culminated in a unique and particular understanding of teaching and teacher education as a profession and calling (Bullough & Stokes, 1994). Some of the knowledge that teacher educators have learned is genius, some flawed, some still too raw to examine even after many years, and much so routine we may hardly notice it at all. As I took up this study, I realized that teacher educator knowledge is often tacit and embodied and emerging; therefore, in order to uncover teacher educator knowledge, a person has to observe and analyze their practices as a teacher educator.

PRESENTATION OF THE PUZZLE

The puzzle that frames this book was a desire to understand what my work in designing a course revealed to me about what I knew as a teacher educator, such as making decisions about course sessions, content, assignments, etc. Uncovering teacher educator knowledge must always be done in a context. This is because teacher educator knowledge is, as I noted earlier, for the most part embodied and tacit. Such embodied knowledge could be vital to the research community when it is uncovered and made explicit. It is important for teacher educators to identify this knowledge, share it within the research conversation in teacher education, and thereby invite other teacher educators to learn from their own teacher educator knowledge in practice. Other than early work by Berry, there is little work that explores teacher educator knowledge.

In the spring of 2020, as I was shifting from in-person to online teaching because of COVID-19, I wondered what I did know as a teacher educator that could inform and support my work in designing an online course for preparing preservice teachers. In addition, I wondered how this knowledge is carried forward or transformed as teacher educators create and enact teaching, not just planning for it. In particular, this inquiry examined my effort to redesign an in-person course that I had taught before to an online format and to specifically examine what the transition revealed about my teacher educator knowledge.

TEACHER EDUCATOR KNOWLEDGE AND S-STEP

In this study focused on the particular (Hamilton & Pinnegar, 2015), I inquired into my understanding of my experience, specifically my teacher educator knowledge, while developing and teaching a course online that I previously taught in a face-to-face format. Building off of Berry's (2007) and Vanassche and Berry's (2020) work, I conceptualized teacher educator knowledge as a "socio-relational accomplishment" that is "shaped and reshaped" through the actions in "particular practice situations" (Vanassche & Berry, 2020, p. 184). Given this focus of teacher educator knowledge as uncovered in practice in a situated context, Vanassche and Berry (2020) argued for the use of self-study of practice as a strategy for uncovering and sharing this kind of knowledge. Not only did their findings provide me with a space to begin my exploration of teacher educator knowledge, their findings also guided my decision to explore the transformation of a course and my thinking during that process. Why this content? Why these readings? Why these activities? Why collaboration? How do I shift to an online context and maintain the integrity of the in-person interaction? These are the questions I was continually aware of as I conducted this study.

The specific practice situation that I wondered about in this narrative self-study was my transition from in-person teaching to online teaching. The research question/wonder that I inquired into was how my transition to online teaching revealed my teacher educator knowledge and commitments. Acknowledging Vanassche and Berry's (2020) assertion that such knowledge would best be revealed as a socio-relational accomplishment that is shaped and reshaped in interaction, my inquiry into this research question was accomplished with the aid of a critical friend.

This inquiry was also undertaken because an important goal of self-study of teacher education practice (S-STEP) is that it must improve practice (see LaBoskey, 2004). In my career as a teacher and teacher educator, I always feel an obligation to improve my practice, but I especially felt this obligation when faced with an online teaching context that was relatively new and unfamiliar. In the transition to teaching in an online setting, I took up the opportunity to examine my knowledge of content, curriculum design, implementation, and instruction.

Therefore, the purpose of this project was to explore teacher educator knowledge and the shifts in teacher educator knowledge that occurred as I, interacting with a critical friend, moved from curriculum-making for in-person courses to curriculum-making for online courses (Clandinin et al., 2009; Connelly & Clandinin, 1988). Postpandemic, in a continued environment of mandated online teacher education, teacher educators are expected to easily and quickly shift their knowledge of curriculum-making to various formats. Transitions are an important time to uncover tacit and embodied understanding. Examining my own teacher educator knowledge makes a contribution to this research conversation in teacher education. Indeed, given the competing contexts of teacher education, it is important to uncover what teacher educator knowledge concerning curriculum design and development emerges in design, implementation, and instruction during the transition from in-person to online contexts.

TEACHER EDUCATOR KNOWLEDGE AND POSSIBLE SITES FOR DISCOVERY

Just like an inquirer has to clearly identify the shape and boundaries of the puzzle they will explore, they also need to carefully consider the context in which the knowledge can be uncovered. While my study examines teacher educator knowledge in the context of the shift to teaching a course online, there are other settings and situations that hold promise for detecting and articulating teacher educator knowledge. Each of the following are potential contexts for future studies of teacher educator knowledge. I will reiterate that for rich self-study, the decisions of which context to explore, the process of inquiry chosen to investigate the puzzle, and the approach to collecting data that will provide the evidence must be strategically thought out.

Program Evaluation Review

As the field of evaluation has grown, three factors helped in legitimizing the field and encouraging it to flourish: a burgeoning economy, a more federal role in education and other policy areas, and a lot more social science graduates (Bullough et al., 2003, pp. 46–47). Thus, with more programs, mandated evaluation, and money to conduct them, this relatively new field of study has spread with enthusiasm. In the current trend of program review, the evaluator's task is to focus on more than just a program's results or characteristics. From here, evaluation questions and measures can be developed to address these key questions.

Many such program reviews are conducted at institutions by internal evaluators, perhaps faculty assigned the task. When asked to participate as an external reviewer, it can take some time as an outsider to become familiar with the structure of the program or surrounding institution, making the process longer or expensive. Yet after analyzing the data collected from stakeholders and other measures, an outside reviewer can often challenge prevailing perspectives in positive ways.

When examining a program's purposes, goals, and sifting through data, the context of an institutional accreditation program review has rich potential for uncovering teacher educator knowledge. According to Pinnegar and Erickson (2009), much of what is discovered during a teacher education program review may not be included in the final report. Indeed, "as reports are constructed and evidence gathered, implicit assumptions, theoretical orientations, policies and procedures, resource allocation and use, are made evident, sometimes painfully so" (p. 152). The process of program review seeks to give stakeholders in institutions a better understanding of how their values and practices are enacted within the program.

Thus, when an institution seeks accreditation or engages in program evaluation, the process is authentic, already occurring, and embedded-in-context. It is an inherently rich setting for potentially identifying valuable insights into teacher educator knowledge, teacher knowledge, and indeed, the held knowledge of all stakeholders including those who may not be as obvious such as "...clinical faculty, teaching adjuncts, secretaries, advisors, support staff, and teacher candidates" (Pinnegar & Erickson, 2009, p. 151). By seeking ways to articulate and document evidence of stated values and goals and even potentially uncover unstated purposes or strongly held beliefs, the collective knowledge of institutional participants could be recognized. Such a focus underscores one of the crucial characteristics of self-study methodology, that findings are aimed at wider improvement of the institution and research community (LaBoskey, 2004).

Teacher Education in an Online Context

In the recent, accelerated transition from in-person to online teacher education, we have not carefully looked at the knowledge teacher educators hold for designing and constructing online courses. It is essential that teacher educators moving out of emergency remote teaching into more stable remote teaching contexts continue to consider, identify, and implement evidence-based approaches as communities of practice, collaboration, and reflection in online teaching contexts. While researchers have asserted what constitutes quality teaching practice for adults in online settings, it is important in teacher education that these practices are not just incorporated into courses but made explicit, modeled, and engaged in by students.

Both nationally and internationally, educational institutions that provide teacher education have increasingly looked to online education as a solution to supporting the learning and development of teachers and teaching (American Association of Colleges for Teacher Education [AACTE], 2013; Cutri, Mena et al., 2020; Dede et al., 2009; Downing & Dyment, 2013; Redmond, 2015; Robinson & Latchem, 2003). Since the 1990s, institutions of higher education have encouraged or mandated more online course offerings (North American Council for Online Learning [NACOL], 2007; Vaughan, 2007), and online learning has also consistently been the most researched topic in educational technology (Kimmons, 2020). Colleges of education have looked to online courses as the solution to economic concerns, access, consistency, and availability (Borko et al., 2010; Dell et al., 2008; Pelliccione et al., 2019). In all stages of teacher preparation, from preservice coursework and field experiences to in-service teacher professional development, online programs have become a common solution (Cutri & Whiting, 2018; Lay et al., 2020).

Teacher educators are increasingly asked to deliver their undergraduate, graduate, and professional development in online formats, often without clear guidelines for quality or sufficient professional support for developing online curriculum, using appropriate technological tools and changing platforms (Bussmann et al., 2017; Cutri & Mena, 2020). In fact, institutions assign teacher educators online courses apparently under the assumption that anyone who has taught in-person courses and has some technological skill can immediately and easily create effective online versions of a course. Indeed, ongoing teacher development programs are often put in place without careful attention to whether and how teacher educators can implement those practices that can bring about changes in teacher practice and thinking (Allman & Pinnegar, 2020).

The move to providing online coursework in teacher education accelerated as institutions responded to the COVID-19 pandemic. Early in March 2020, most universities in the United States sent students home and within days had transitioned classes to online (Arum & Stevens, 2020; Hechinger & Lorin, 2020; McMurtrie, 2020). With the onset of the pandemic, teacher educators were almost immediately required to shift from in-person to online instruction. This has led some people to differentiate online instruction developed before the pandemic with the emergency remote teaching (ERT) that took place beginning in the spring of 2020 in the United States (Hodges et al., 2020; Milman, 2020). The COVID-19 pandemic increased the demand for effective online teacher education that could be designed, implemented, and assessed with fidelity (Ferdig et al., 2020; Hartshorne et al., 2020).

As teacher educators seek to create optimum curriculum for teacher education in online contexts, they are confronted with limitations and concerns. It is equally important that the pedagogy preservice teachers engage in during teacher education should both mirror and provide preservice teachers with experience in the pedagogies they need to practice when teaching students (Cutri, Whiting et al., 2020). Further, other characteristics identified as hallmarks of teacher learning such as reflection (Brookfield, 2017; Moon, 1999), field experiences, collaboration, and ongoing interaction across time require serious investigation in how they may be implemented successfully in online contexts (Desimone, 2009; Opfer & Pedder, 2011; Penuel et al., 2007).

8   *How Can We frame Inquiry Into Teacher Educator Knowledge?*

In a postpandemic environment of in-person, blended, and continued online teacher education, in which teacher educators are expected to easily and quickly transfer their knowledge of curriculum-making to an online context, the research community needs to better understand what shifts in teacher educator knowledge will be most efficacious for teacher educators engaging in moving their course to online formats. Yet, the research community does not have codified accounts of this kind of knowledge (Vanassche & Berry, 2020). Seeking local, authentic answers to some of these dilemmas and uncovering this knowledge could make an important contribution to the research conversation in teacher education.

Program Revitalization and Redesign

During program redesign, many of the tensions identified in Chapter 2 must be negotiated. In particular, is the program university-based, and what is the program's participation within the larger institution? Is the program approach to teacher preparation as training or as education? How much teacher education coursework should be required? How will field experiences be designed? Organizational restructuring is expensive and difficult, and the question of whose ideas on teacher preparation are going to be the foundation must be considered. Darling-Hammond (2004) described what needs were identified during the Stanford Teacher Education Program revitalization. While still building on strengths, the program sought to be more anchored in professional standards and a "common vision of good teaching," a better understanding of how to teach challenging content to diverse learners, stronger links between theory and practice, and strengthened partnerships with local schools and teachers. Careful study was given to coursework and major assignments drew on information from other classes as well as field experiences.

In this revitalization process, there are numerous possibilities for collecting data that could uncover teacher and teacher educator knowledge. For example, some of the data sources that were collected and studied during the Stanford program redesign were: teacher candidates' learning and performance from objective tests, observations from field experiences, particular research studies focused on the teaching of English language learners, reflections, surveys, interviews, pre- and post-tests, work samples, observations of teacher candidate practice over time, graduate surveys, and data from employers (Darling-Hammond, 2004, p. 15). In addition, there are numerous opportunities for collaboration in program revitalization, since such an endeavor is never undertaken by one individual. Therefore, while working with others, this could be a potentially fruitful approach for designing a self-study in which collaborators could examine the teacher educator knowledge they hold as they evaluate and consider the learning and needs of teacher candidates and school partnerships.

Collaborative Self-Studies With Colleagues Around Important Books

One researched strategy for teachers to connect and engage in professional learning is to read a professional book together. In the findings of one study by

Burbank et al. (2010), the practicing teachers reported that the books "...provided a starting point from which to begin important discussions about teaching and professional dilemmas" (p. 64). While the logistics of getting a group of professionals together to meet is inherently tricky, participants often reflect that the sharing of a book leads to better relationships and important learning. The most successful groups are usually structured with a regular time, meeting place (including online gatherings), and a facilitator. Meeting in a supportive environment with other teacher educators, or even with an interdisciplinary group, could be a setting that would uncover teacher educator knowledge.

Along with deciding which book to read, the design of the question is also a crucial element. One example of how to approach a guiding question comes from Ritchhart et al. (2011) as they describe cognitive strategies for making thinking visible. One of their strategies (Connect, Extend, Challenge) invites participants to connect what they've read to something they know about, extend their thinking to new questions or ideas, and describe what was challenging in the reading, identifying what they still wonder about. It is useful in a collaborative self-study, and perhaps a book discussion setting, to have one anchoring question that researchers can keep circling back to, for instance, "What connections, new ideas, or challenging thoughts am I having and how might they reveal my underlying teacher educator knowledge?" (Pinnegar et al., 2005).

Such questions as how to collect the data, what data to collect, and how to come together are clearly also important considerations. When beginning a collaborative self-study, it is imperative to set the boundaries, to discuss and agree upon the decisions and parameters about participation and goals. Who will do the work? Who will get the credit?

MY OWN SELF-STUDY OF TEACHER EDUCATOR KNOWLEDGE

Thus far, I have introduced myself as a teacher educator living and working in the mountain west of the United States. I have presented the puzzle, or research question, that guided this study. It was, "What does my transition to online teaching reveal about my teacher educator knowledge?" I briefly explained the role of Self-Study of Teacher Education Practice (S-STEP) as a methodological approach to uncovering my tacit knowledge as a teacher educator. I have posited other possible sites and scenarios for uncovering teacher educator knowledge. Now, I will outline the remaining chapters in the book.

Chapter 2 begins with the question, "What do we know about teacher education and how do we use that knowledge?" In this chapter, a brief history of teacher education in the United States is given, and tensions at the heart of teacher education are explored. The tension between schools of education within institutions of higher education influences decisions about curriculum choices, stances on rigor, and program design and delivery. The tension between whether teacher preparation should operate from a position of training or a position of education is examined. Such decisions influence how teacher candidates are treated – as novices with some tips and tricks to acquire, or as preservice teachers with beliefs and thinking of their own. The tension between university coursework and preservice field experiences is also examined, in particular the pull between what is important to be taught at the university and how much time teacher candidates should spend in schools. Since I am a teacher educator operating within these tensions, it is a useful investigation to consider the decisions I made in a particular situation of practice and how, in my study, I sought to understand not just the knowledge uncovered but the obligations and commitments to students, colleagues, communities, and even myself.

Chapter 3 asks the question, "What methodology and accompanying strategies allow us to uncover teacher educator knowledge?" In this chapter, I provide a detailed description of my methodological stance, data collection process, and analysis methods. I begin by explaining my choice of Self-Study of Teacher Education Practice (S-STEP) as a methodology because it positions researchers to examine their own practice and explore beliefs and moral and political values, thereby adding to the research conversation of teacher education, and also turn what we learn into improvement of practice. Although self-study of practice is a methodology without a proscribed set of method, other methods of qualitative analysis are employed in self-study. A variety of qualitative methods such as dialogue, critical friendship, exemplars, and analytic narrative vignettes were selected and implemented in order to collect, organize, analyze, and present the data. Researcher positionality and ethics are also discussed in this chapter. I end with a discussion on trustworthiness and rigor in relation to methodological approaches and strategies employed in qualitative research, especially inherently vulnerable nature of self-study research and the responsibility of protecting all participants and researchers.

In Chapter 4, the guiding question is, "How can analytic narrative vignettes allow complex representation of data?" I then provide a detailed explanation of how analytical narrative vignettes were used in the study. Certain understandings, or strands, of my own teacher educator knowledge emerged in the process of planning for, teaching, and reflecting on an online course for preservice teachers. In order to reveal and then analyze those strands, evidence for the strands of teacher educator knowledge was exemplified by through analytic narrative vignettes based on the data. The process of creating vignettes raised the status of this evidence to exemplars (Mishler, 1990). In order to make the purpose of vignettes and their composition clear, I give a theoretical case for creating exemplars in qualitative data analysis. Then I explain the procedure by providing excerpted samples from the original data and then walking through analysis and my developing thinking about the strands of teacher educator knowledge. I also include some of the decision-making that went into composing a vignette and show how the process of composing vignettes and then unpacking them for analysis served as an additional step in the analysis.

The title of Chapter 5 poses the question, "What does the Planning Vignette reveal about teacher educator knowledge?" In this chapter, seven strands of teacher educator knowledge are presented, with a particular focus on the Planning Vignette. For the purpose of examining, analyzing, and presenting the data and findings, I divided the data into three phases: planning for the course, teaching the course, and reflecting on the course. I composed an exemplar for each of these three phases that captured the data in the form of a narrative vignette. The Planning Vignette offers a narrative picture of two colleagues sitting at a kitchen table preparing to teach a course on Integrating Content and Language and Literacy for English language learners in the spring of 2020. Then, I examine the strands of teacher educator knowledge revealed in the narrative.

In Chapter 6, the seven strands of teacher educator knowledge are further examined, with a particular focus on the Teaching Vignette. The guiding question is, "What does the Teaching Vignette reveal about teacher educator knowledge?" The seven strands are: *Content Knowledge, Fixed and Fluid Elements, Knowledge of Milieu, Pedagogical Intent, Preservice Teacher Knowledge and Belief, Value and Fragility of Relationships,* and *Theory Matters.* The Teaching Vignette is a narrative representation of two colleagues teaching an online course to preservice teachers on Integrating Content and Language and Literacy for English language learners in the spring of 2020. The strands are revealed in the statements made by the professors, in assignment design and course decisions, and through interactions with students. I conclude by summarizing how each of the strands of teacher educator knowledge was revealed in explicit and implicit ways and how they influenced each other.

In Chapter 7, I ask, "What Does the Reflecting Vignette Reveal About Teacher Educator Knowledge?" Through an analysis of the Reflecting Vignette, the seven strands of teacher educator knowledge are revealed and examined. This vignette represents the data gathered after teaching, including debriefing meetings that occurred with my co-instructor immediately following a class session, as well as final reflections engaged in after the course was completed. Each of the three vignettes was intended to represent the major understandings about teacher educator knowledge but not necessarily include every example from the data, simply those that provided the strongest evidence. At the stage of reflection, the strands were solidified and robust. I conclude the analysis of the Reflecting Vignette with a summary of how each of the seven strands of teacher educator knowledge was revealed in explicit and implicit ways, and how they influenced each other.

In Chapter 8, I explore individually the seven strands of teacher educator knowledge. The question that guides this chapter is, "What are the strands of teacher educator knowledge embedded across the vignettes?" In the previous three chapters, when I analyzed the vignettes, the strands all became evident, some more apparently than others. For this chapter, in order to communicate these strands of teacher educator knowledge in my transition to teaching online, I defined each strand generally and showed how it operates in terms of planning, teaching, and reflecting. I noted episodes of relationship building, preservice teacher beliefs, my engagement with students and with the content, and my core attention to theory, especially my understanding about sociocultural learning, learning online and using technology, and the interplay of the commonplaces of teacher, student, milieu, and curriculum in action. I conclude with an explanation of how this knowledge influenced my identity and informed my commitment as a teacher educator.

In Chapter 9, I pose the question, "What Does this Study Contribute To Our Understanding About Teacher Education?" In this chapter, I restate the need to develop an understanding of teacher educator knowledge. I reflect on my purpose of coming to understand my decision-making as a curriculum-maker and conclude this study was a successful way to develop and contribute more sophisticated understandings to the concept of teacher educator knowledge. I also discuss the significance of context in choosing sites for investigating teacher educator knowledge. I learned from my own experience in shifting a class I had frequently taught face to face to an online format that this shift was the perfect site for capturing decisions made and data generated around those decisions. Indeed, this site provided an ideal situation under which teacher educator knowledge could be uncovered and personally examined using a self-study of practice methodology. Finally, I revisit the strands of teacher educator knowledge, highlighting some important connections and insights that were explored using the vignettes on planning, teaching, and reflecting. An important theme throughout this chapter is the value of recognizing the obligations and commitments to students, colleagues, communities, and myself that were revealed as integral and interrelated in the strands of teacher educator knowledge.

In Chapter 10, I pose the question, "What Are The implications Of Studies Of Teacher Educator Knowledge For Teacher Education?" In this study, the context of moving a class I had previously taught face to face to an online format was an important site for revealing teacher educator knowledge with some strands being especially valuable for carrying out the goals and purposes of the course. Because of this, there is an obvious invitation for other researchers to investigate teacher educator knowledge in online settings and in other settings as well. In addition, because teacher education is fundamentally relational, there are moral and ethical concerns that are always present. Studies to examine how the strands of teacher educator knowledge may reveal the ways in which moral and ethical concerns shape and constrain teacher educator knowledge could lead to a deeper and more nuanced understanding of how the moral and ethical are involved in teacher educator knowledge and decision-making. Implications for programs and practitioners are further explored.

WHAT DO WE KNOW ABOUT TEACHER EDUCATION, AND HOW DO WE USE THAT KNOWLEDGE?

ABSTRACT

It is useful to approach an understanding of teacher education, particularly in the United States, by looking at the roots and aims of teacher preparation. In this chapter, three main tensions are explored. First, there is tension in the positioning of teacher education as it resides in institutions of higher education. Second, an ongoing tension is the question of teacher preparation as training or as education. Third, there is always tension between the balance of teacher education coursework and field experiences. As these tensions play out in various teacher education programs, we can see the influence of each in the structure and processes involved in the program. Decisions regarding these tensions become highly visible in the move toward online teaching and online teacher education. While these tensions cannot necessarily be tidied or completely reconciled, there is evidence that teacher educators are committed to bringing forth best practices, connecting theory and practice and reflection, in their practice and in their scholarship. This chapter ends with an overview of teacher educator knowledge, its roots in teacher knowledge, including theoretical, methodological, and pedagogical considerations, and how teacher educator knowledge informs online education and influences the ways in which we prepare teachers postpandemic.

Keywords: Teacher education; higher education; normal schools; online teacher education; field experiences; theory practice divide; teacher knowledge; knowledge of teaching; teacher educator knowledge

In the second edition of the *Handbook of Research on Teacher Education*, Ducharme and Ducharme (1996) stated that there is often confusion in the teacher education research landscape regarding what it is we know and how we use what we know. They recommended the investigation of the preparation and experience of teacher educators as an area of needed research; specifically, they recommended inquiry into teacher educators' understandings of pedagogy, attitudes toward learners, and self-concepts of teacher educators themselves.

Exploring Teacher Educator Knowledge
Advances in Research on Teaching, Volume 48, 13–34
Copyright © 2025 Celina Dulude Lay
Published under exclusive licence by Emerald Publishing Limited
ISSN: 1479-3687/doi:10.1108/S1479-368720240000048002

Researchers since this time have directly and indirectly addressed these questions using a range of methodologies but mostly qualitative research (Clandinin & Husu, 2017; Loughran & Hamilton, 2016).

What follows is an overview of what we know about teacher education both nationally and internationally, although with a North American emphasis. This overview includes ongoing tensions in teacher education, how these tensions have been resolved in online teacher education, and how teacher educators are currently using what they know. Then I consider what we know about teacher educator knowledge, including theoretical, methodological, and pedagogical considerations, how teacher educator knowledge informs online education, and how teacher educators are currently using what they know to prepare teachers postpandemic.

OVERVIEW OF TEACHER EDUCATION

There has always been tension at the heart of teacher education (Sikula, 1996, pp. xv–xxiii). These are ongoing dilemmas that emerge from the conflicting aims of education, teacher education, and teaching. Yet, instead of raging at intractable, irreconcilable ideas, it is more productive for teacher educators to approach these tensions "as elements that are necessary, even enjoyable, for the growth and learning that they bring" (Berry, 2007, p. 42). The first tension to be explored is the problematic positioning of teacher education within institutions of higher education. A second tension revolves around enacting teacher education – with approaches to preparing teachers that lean toward teacher training or more toward teacher education. A third dilemma addresses the conflict between university coursework and public school field experiences – which are more important or how much is desired of each. Despite these continuing tensions, the research indicates that the prevailing commitments in teacher education are to turn toward scholarship, education, and an integration of theory and practice and reflection (Kitchen, 2020). These commitments and associated prevailing best practices are currently being negotiated in teacher education on a global scale.

Tension of Teacher Education Within Institutions

The first tension is the problematic positioning of teacher education within institutions of higher education. Both nationally and internationally, faculty in schools of education have difficulty being respected as scholars (Cochran-Smith & Fries, 2005; Davey, 2013; Goodlad, 1990a; Lanier & Little, 1986). Preparing to be a teacher still does not inspire the same kind of status and admiration as a similar student preparing for business, medicine, or law, even when assessments of preservice teacher knowledge in comparison to other disciplines indicate that preservice teachers' level of knowledge is the same as those who are preparing to work in other disciplines (Darling-Hammond et al., 2017). Similarly, faculty who are preparing those teachers do not inspire the same kind of status and admiration as faculty of other fields at institutions of higher education, even though

EXPLORING TEACHER EDUCATOR KNOWLEDGE

many of these institutions only exist since they were originally organized as normal schools with the purpose of preparing teachers (Davey, 2013).

The more scholarly and recognized teacher educators become, the more likely their research is to drift from the practical and useful and become increasingly more distanced from teacher education (Goodlad et al., 1990). Also, as teacher educators become recognized for scholarship, the less likely the institution is to allow them to engage in teacher education, which again relegates them to positions distanced from and less practical and useful to schools (Clifford & Guthrie, 1990; Pinnegar, 2017). Indeed, there is constant public skepticism about the value of a teacher educator's credentials and how teacher education can translate to both practical skill and knowledge (Davey, 2013; Garbett, 2013). As summed up by Clifford and Guthrie (1990), "Schools of education are perpetual targets for criticism" (p. 37).

Social and political tension in teacher education can be traced to the beginnings of teacher preparation in the United States. Formalized teacher education in the United States emerged almost 200 years ago in response to the urbanization of communities and with the creation of normal schools in most states (Schwartz, 1996). As communities sought for more and better teachers for their children, normal schools opened and began to professionalize teaching, often at the high school level and sometimes including some time spent at a laboratory school housed in a school of education campus (Clifford & Guthrie, 1990). These first teacher preparation institutions were state-operated. Some normal schools were didactic in design, with explicit training on *when* and *how* to do *what*, without delving into *why*, and others, like the Dewey schools, focused more on a teacher education approach (Ducharme & Ducharme, 1996; Goodlad, 1984).

After World War I, normal schools evolved to include courses in pedagogy, learning theories, and discipline knowledge. The introduction, therefore, of courses in philosophy, mathematics, etc., enabled the normal schools were absorbed or changed into state colleges or universities (Clifford & Guthrie, 1990; Schwartz, 1996). At many of these institutions of higher education, prospective teachers were required to take a series of courses, which emerged as a blend of liberal arts requirements and criteria developed state by state for accreditation. Therefore, from the beginning, aims of teacher education have been influenced by state directives for schooling, a need in both rural and urban communities for teachers, and the evolving formation of institutions of higher education.

When *A Nation at Risk* was published in 1983 (National Commission on Excellence in Education [NCEE], 1983), teacher educators absorbed the blows for the perceived failing state of education in the United States. More than a decade later, in another federal report, *What Matters Most: Teaching for America's Future* (National Commission on Teaching and America's Future [NCTAF], 1996) advocated better teacher preparation and professional development but with a market-based agenda designed with standards in mind and the power to close down underperforming teacher education programs. According to Bullough (2019):

16   *What Do We know About Teacher Education?*

> ... the report was written as though nothing had been done to improve teacher education since the publication of *A Nation at Risk*. The message was beginning to sink in: there was no way to satisfy the critics of teacher education who, by exploiting a deep-seated historic American faith in the reformative and restorative powers of education, shifted onto teachers and teacher educators the blame for the results of poorly conceived and sometimes mean-spirited social and economic policies that encouraged all sorts of mischief for children, families, schools, and the wider society. (p. 36)

Indeed, through many presidents, the United States federal government has invaded every state with reform efforts for schools and teacher education such as *No Child Left Behind* and *Race to the Top* that are based in an aggressive neoliberal political agenda (Bullough, 2019).

In the 2000s, state-sponsored teacher education continued to be portrayed as failing, and particularly in the United States, government funding was more likely to be provided to private programs than to university programs (Zeichner, 2018). Accreditation by the National Council for Accreditation of Teacher Education (NCATE) was often difficult even at schools with established reputations for quality teacher preparation (Bullough et al., 2003).

In this environment, some recent voices for education reform omit teacher education as even having a role in the process of reimagining "what schools could be" (e.g., Dintersmith, 2018). In his book, Dintersmith visited and reported successes he observed in numerous schools, but it never seemed to occur to him that these innovative approaches he lauded were probably based on research conducted by teacher educators. Nor did he consider the role teacher educators in higher education institutions may have played in supporting teachers in developing these practices either in preservice or in-service professional learning capacities.

There are other ways that lawmakers and stakeholders undercut traditional teacher education programs while simultaneously holding them accountable for perceived failures in student learning. The current trend in most states and even internationally is for some teachers to have the option to receive their credentials through alternative paths or be assigned to teach out of field (Mulvihill & Martin, 2019; Van Overschelde & Piatt, 2020). Even though most teachers were then and still are prepared in college and university programs, these programs receive less and less funding from their respective states. Yet colleges of teacher education, unlike alternative routes to teaching, are still charged with producing measurable results and evidence of high-performance (National Research Council [NRC], 2010).

While teacher education was historically looked to as a way for governments to establish and regulate a teaching force, some countries have increased regulatory measures on teacher education to a breaking point. These wider policy pressures have influenced teacher education within institutions of higher education to be managed in a more market-driven approach with pressure to produce results and provide quality assurance (Brown et al., 2016; Yuan, 2016). Within their countries and institutions, teacher educators occupy tricky spaces of increased mandates and decreased resources. They are often required to conduct research that is respected rather than relevant, collaborate richly with

EXPLORING TEACHER EDUCATOR KNOWLEDGE 17

stakeholders, schools, and in-service teachers, and provide "just what is needed" to prospective teachers. Unique to teacher education, except perhaps schools of business, it is assumed that those who teach teachers ought to have been successful as teachers or educators. But at the same time when they come as academics to the university, they are coming later in their careers and in their lives than the cohort of people they went to undergraduate education with and have to start all over again with building an academic career. Their successes and tenure and reputation as a teacher or educator are irrelevant in this greater higher education context. Ultimately, the many ways teacher educators participate in preparing teachers are complex and undervalued.

Pressured by a market-based agenda and even by student demands for online courses (Miller & Ribble, 2010), there is a sense that shifting to online formats both in K-12 settings and in higher education is a simple thing. The popularity and explosive growth of online teacher education often outpaces rigorous empirical research. The reality is that the work of producing online courses is demanding on time and resources, and there is limited opportunity for systematic empirical research that could provide guidelines for improving the quality. Additionally, a key participant and critical presence to the success of an online teacher learning program, the technology support expert, is rarely visible or represented in the research (Lay et al., 2020).

Even still, because of increased demands, many colleges of teacher education have looked to online teacher education as a solution in the face of dwindling financial investment. This popularity has been motivated in part by the potential of technology to address issues of access and delivery, but particularly cost (AACTE, 2013; Cutri & Whiting, 2018; Latchem & Robinson, 2003). Thus, this dilemma of the problematic positioning of teacher education within institutions of higher education directly influences the current turn toward online teacher education. In the research, there is limited investigation of the ways that moving online may require a shift in teacher educator thinking or an expansion of knowledge and pedagogies. Therefore, it is important to have local studies that formally inquire into teacher educator knowledge and the shifts that occur in teacher educators' knowledge concerning curriculum design and development as they transition from designing and implementing instruction in-person to online contexts.

Tension of Teacher Preparation as Training Versus Education

The second dilemma revolves around enacting teacher education – whether the approach to preparing teachers should be teacher training or teacher education. Over the years, teacher education has sometimes leaned toward a training approach to prepare teachers with a set of articulated competencies. Other times, it has followed an education approach which supports preservice teachers in building on what they already know and involves theoretical and practical experiences with schools and students. A training approach to teacher education implies that the skills needed to teach well are completely definable. In fact, the new orientation to teacher preparation practices is based on the assumption that teachers can be trained on signature practices (Ball & Forzani, 2009). This question has been deeply debated as many researchers have made assertions about what knowledge and skills beginning teachers should have acquired in their teacher preparation programs (Cochran-Smith & Zeichner, 2005).

Due to the early and ongoing myriad of stakeholders and many voices trying to distill what teachers need to know, approaches to teacher education are not easily agreed upon. Initially, in the United States, normal schools established that teacher preparation should include content knowledge, pedagogical knowledge, and application and practice of both. In the wake of the Industrial Revolution and in North America experiencing a massive immigration from Europe, governments invested in teacher education to educate the masses in the most efficient way (Altenbaugh & Underwood, 1990). While Dewey (1929/2013) endorsed teacher education that was based in theory and centered in experience, historically what became prevalent were teacher education courses slanted toward sorting children for efficient mass schooling and smooth entry into the economic structure:

> ... exemplified by the growth of standardized testing and distinct vocational programs to at least the 1920s, and curriculum and instruction driven by frequent assessment of microskill attainment – the latter a tradition dating to the earliest common schools, given a great boost by the competency-based education movement in the late 1960s and 1970s. Undergirding this particular values orientation of schooling have been rigid grouping practices – by grade levels, perceived ability, presumed job future, handicapping condition, and even behavior – that eloquent but drowned-out voices have been decrying since at least the turn of the century. (Levin, 1990, p. 52)

Levin's description sums up the tension about a completely skill-based, competence-slanted teacher education oriented to training. Such training is fundamentally filled with restraint and control.

This trend is ongoing and not isolated to the United States. For example, Gage (1972) asserted the need to articulate the teaching process "into various component activities" (p. 20) which has been taken up again in the signature pedagogy movement (see Ball & Forzani, 2009). In Canada, for example, Clandinin (2000) described such a set of component skills as knowledge for teaching but cautioned that teacher education programs only oriented to a knowledge for teaching may result in detached, fragmented bits that must be transmitted. In contrast, Clandinin (2000) has argued for an alternative view of "teacher knowledge," wherein "teachers hold knowledge that comes from experience, is learned in context, and is expressed in practice" (p. 29). According to Pantić and Wubbles (2012), teacher educators in many countries feel the tension of a culture focused on curriculum (in which preservice teachers are amassing skills) and an opposing culture more in the German Didaktik tradition, in which "the essential aim of teaching is 'Bildung' – unfolding by learning a process of the formation of the student self and linking it to the world" (p. 65).

Like the Didaktik tradition, others have long advocated for a more holistic approach that supports preservice teachers in having experiences to practice theory and theorize practice (Clandinin et al., 1993; Darling-Hammond, 2006; Doyle, 1990).

EXPLORING TEACHER EDUCATOR KNOWLEDGE

Holt-Reynolds' (1991, 1992) research provided clear evidence that the knowledge and beliefs preservice teachers have that they bring to their teacher preparation program influence their learning. This has implications for the knowledge base for teaching and also for decisions about teacher education curriculum and pedagogies.

Questions about both a knowledge base for teaching and assessments for beginning teachers are ongoing, as researchers have tried to establish exactly what beginning teachers should know. This has shaped the more recent curriculum of teacher education, the accreditation requirements of teacher accreditation institutions, and teacher assessments. Although she advocates a more holistic education approach, Clandinin (2000) clearly described a training orientation when she stated:

> Knowledge and skills [more recently decomposed practices] are assumed to be possessions, held and performed by people in objective ways ... We teach how to plan a lesson, a unit, a theme; how to discipline a child; how to conduct oneself within the professional code of ethics; how to convey a particular science concept ... In each course or part of a program, a set of knowledge, skills, and attitudes is presented, and students are tested to see if they have acquired the set. Student teaching is the time for students to apply those bits of knowledge in practice. (pp. 28–29)

Clandinin argued that under this "knowledge for teaching" approach to teacher education, the content knowledge and skills for teaching it are divided out across the teacher education curriculum. It is during field experiences that preservice teachers are to integrate that knowledge, and almost invariably, at this point, teacher educators are absent or focused more on assessment than development.

In a review of literature, Kagan (1992) proposed an approach to teacher preparation that pointed toward itemized training. In rebuttal to Kagan's review, Grossman (1992) expressed concern that teacher preparation cannot be divided neatly into classroom management tips and study of teaching and learning. She named other current research that supported the inclusion of moral dimensions, reflection on practice, and expansion of past prior knowledge and experience to teacher preparation.

Traditional evidence for making a judgment about a preservice teacher's readiness to teach has long been based on proxies such as completion of coursework or grades from evaluations (Mayer, 2013). Ball and Forzani (2009) aligned themselves with a micro-skill training approach by advocating that we identify core practices and train preservice teachers to enact first the elements and then the whole practice. According to Ball and Forzani (2009), the work of a teacher is specialized and requires professional training. Indeed, "most adults do not naturally develop the ability to perform the tasks required of teachers" (p. 500). Even more recently, in her book *Teaching Core Practices in Teacher Education*, Grossman (2018) has shifted her stance and voiced this view, advocating for the explicit teaching of core practices for preservice and novice teachers by breaking down pedagogical skills into their component parts and then training them.

Since the 1990s, governments, schools, and other policymakers have concentrated more than ever before on improving the quality of teacher education (United Nations Educational, Scientific and Cultural Organization [UNESCO], 2007). Many countries with growing economies are currently looking to teacher education to enable them to establish and regulate a teaching force. However, many of these programs are pressured by top-down government and institutional directives, which often results in attempts to break down teaching knowledge into itemized lists.

At the same time, there continues to be a strong group of proponents that seek to prepare teachers by identifying their strengths and building from there. This capacity-oriented framework does not stop at academic coursework but also includes opportunities for preservice teachers to learn methods of inquiry and reflection and experience the importance of developing relationships with families and communities (Abu El-Haj & Rubin, 2009). Further, practices and assessments for preparing teachers in issues of social justice and equity cannot successfully be broken down into micro-skills. Teacher preparation that engages preservice teachers in differentiating instruction for diverse learners often begins with engaging preservice teachers in identifying their own cultural, social, and linguistic capital.

Adding to the difficulty of how teacher preparation should be oriented – as training or as education – is the ongoing debate of whether teachers are born or made. The nativist myth adds to the tension because many stakeholders, teachers included, conclude that being a good teacher is an inherent quality, and all a teacher may need from teacher education is to acquire a few tricks of the trade and a university degree for certification (Ball & Forzani, 2009; Darling-Hammond, 2006; Scott & Dinham, 2008). In contrast, both Goodlad (1984) and Bullough et al. (1991) made the argument that while some teacher candidates may enter the program with better dispositions or skills, any person can be educated to be a teacher.

Training and education are often presented as dichotomous tensions, but according to Bullough (2019), "training is not a substitute for education, but teacher education without attention to training brings its own serious defects" (p. 50). As Pinnegar (1997) explained, no matter how competently a preservice teacher can "perform a skill or exhibit a particular disposition which we require, when they leave us it will most likely drop from their repertoire unless there is a place in their understanding of experience (what it will be like as they become a teacher) to which it can connect" (p. 44). Thus, this dilemma of how to treat the balance of training and education is a pertinent one to consider for designing high-quality teacher education programs.

It is in this context that institutions of higher education began offering more online classes, and researchers began investigating the range of pedagogies available in online formats (Garrison et al., 2004; Vaughan, 2007). As online teacher education expanded, researchers began to study drawbacks and affordances of preparing teachers online and question how educative their classes could be (Dell et al., 2008; McQuiggan, 2007; Vaughan, 2007). Thus, the tension of teaching as training or as education is also present in online teacher preparation course development.

Online teacher education that aligns with a teaching-as-training orientation is popular for many reasons. First, online programs allow institutions to increase the size and scale of their programs, in order to provide teacher education or teacher professional development to more people. Indeed, as long as students have sufficient digital access, more teachers can be prepared from anywhere, even reaching remote locations in need of more and better trained teachers. Online students are also easily evaluated since online courses require students to post information which is then readily available. Other data are also easily accessed such as time spent online, repeated surveys, annotated lesson plans, etc. Further, it is appealing to be able to order online workshops or training that can be designed to meet specific educational needs (Lay et al., 2020). The ease of producing checklist-type coursework online (which is frequently demanded by students as well) adds to the growing popularity of online offerings. In short, many of the relevant pressures that have led institutions to choose online formats lend themselves to a teacher training orientation – teacher preparation that can be distilled to a set of skills (Dahal & Pangeni, 2019; Hew & Brush, 2007; Wambugu, 2018).

In contrast, many in teacher education research also investigate how online teacher education can include spaces for reflection, discussion, and engaging preservice teachers in building knowledge that is political, moral, and ethical, while also modeling effective online teaching practices (Dell et al., 2008; Grant et al., 2018; Mills et al., 2009). There is growing evidence that in online teacher learning, participatory or learning community practices have worked better than some content-driven approaches, especially in the area of online teacher professional development (e.g., Masters et al., 2012; So et al., 2009; Wang & Lu, 2012). It is perhaps more of a challenge to approach online teacher education as capacity-building rather than competence-based, but designers and researchers committed to sociocultural teaching practices are investigating online course design in order to choose what skills, applications, or teacher engagement strategies will most effectively influence desired teacher learning and support preservice teachers in developing in sociocultural pedagogy (Hambacher et al., 2018; Murphy & Pinnegar, 2018).

Entire online teacher education programs or a few online courses have been the norm at universities and for teacher preparation for 20 years. Research and investigation of effective ways of conceptualizing online teacher professional learning have not yet caught up to the demand. Given the circumstances of the COVID-19 pandemic, employing methodologies and methods that acknowledge the complexity and situatedness of preparing teachers online is particularly crucial as conditions of crisis, and even trauma, characterize the design and implementation of online teacher education. For this reason, it is important, perhaps more than ever before, for teacher educators to investigate their own teacher educator knowledge as they develop and teach courses in online contexts.

Tension of Teacher Education Coursework and Field Experiences

A third tension in teacher preparation addresses the value of university coursework in relation to public school field experiences. This tension emerges from long-standing discussions of the theory/practice divide (Schwab, 1960/1978) and the previous discussion of the fragmentation of the components of knowledge of teaching as opposed to a more holistic education approach. Even those teacher educators who advocate a core-skill, teacher training approach do not completely discard a commitment in the field to scholarship or to the study of educational, critical, and pedagogical theory (Ball & Forzani, 2009; Grossman, 2018).

Historically, there has been a perceived disconnect between university courses in teacher education and field experiences (Zeichner, 2010). Pinnegar (2017) labeled this a conundrum, describing how during field experiences, preservice teachers are no longer in a student relationship with their teacher educators, so they naturally look to the teachers they are working with in schools for advice from those living in practice. This is often when content taught in university courses could either be taken up or rejected, and "who preservice teachers seek out to solve their need to perform well is determined by how they label the press of experience they are currently navigating (coursework or field experience)" (p. 213). Clandinin's (2000) distinction between knowledge of teaching and teacher knowledge highlights this tension, indicating that the education of preservice teachers begins, in their view, not with theory they learned in the university but with their experiences in the field. In this context, the pieces of teacher training become useful only insofar as preservice teachers connect those skills to their developing teacher knowledge during field experiences (pp. 29–30).

Those who are in support of teacher education that is more clinically oriented often express an aversion to theory (Kagan, 1992; Zeichner, 2018). Preservice teachers themselves characteristically value practice over theory, finding irrelevant such courses as educational philosophy (Goodlad, 1990b). Yet, as stated by Clift and Brady (2005), research has borne out the importance of a convergence of practice with theory along with "planned, guided, and sustained interactions with pupils (children and adolescents) within early field and student teaching settings" (p. 316). However, for that to occur, teacher educators themselves have to have accurate knowledge of both practice and theory and bring those experiences together for preservice teachers (Martin, 2017). Because of the many social and political factors driving educational choices, it is impossible ever to resolve decisions about how to develop practice and theory during field experiences, how many and how early these field experiences occur, and how much time and attention teacher educators have to be devoted to each at any given time in a program.

One of the difficulties for responding to this tension is that preservice teachers are often confronted with a leap from university coursework to field experience. Many educational theories do not make this leap to practical application easily (Kimmons & Johnstun, 2019). There is often a chasm from learning a theory, a conceptual model that allows individuals to understand their experience, to applying that theory in practice and seeing immediately how that conceptual

EXPLORING TEACHER EDUCATOR KNOWLEDGE

model can be applied in particular situations. For example, in the field of educational technology, Kimmons et al. (2020) stated:

> Teaching technology integration requires teacher educators to grapple with (a) constantly changing, politically impacted professional requirements, (b) continuously evolving educational technology resources, and (c) varying needs across content disciplines and contexts. Teacher educators cannot foresee how their students may be expected to use educational technologies in the future or how technologies will change during their careers. (p. 176)

Kimmons et al. then proposed a model designed to help preservice teachers carry forward concepts learned in theory and then apply in future practice in "meaningful, effective, and sustainable ways" (p. 176). The purpose of the model as a tool for attending to new uses of technology in teaching is represented as a matrix with three dimensions on each axis. On the x axis, teacher's use of tech replaces (R), amplifies (A), or transforms (T) traditional practice. On the y axis, students' relationship to tech is passive (P), interactive (I), or creative (C). When these components are integrated in a three-by-three matrix, it provides nine points to critically examine the use of technology to promote learning.

Theories of social justice and critical race theory in education provide another example of this tension between coursework and field experience. Investigations into how these theories are enacted in practice are usually about the failure of preservice teachers to embrace these practices. Zeichner (2018) has argued that while so many teacher education programs in the United States. declare social justice as a major focus of their programs, these programs do not actually transform the practices and develop commitments in preservice teachers to enact the theory they learn, such as culturally responsive teaching. Teacher educators have an important task to explore their tacit knowledge in this area and uncover their knowledge of how university coursework and field experiences could be linked in ways that inform and transform preservice teacher thinking and practice.

Another area of resistance to integrating theory and practice on the part of preservice teachers comes from inquiry approaches to teaching within the various disciplines. Again, this has been an ongoing problem with most studies reporting the failure of preservice teachers to fully embrace these practices as they become teachers. For example, Klein (2004) reported that preservice teachers are able to "speak the new truths" about inquiry methods of teaching mathematics but in practice and action are not able to establish these methods and pedagogies with learners.

Further, in science education, preservice science teachers have found it challenging and even overwhelming to enact effective inquiry methods while also developing a complex conceptual knowledge of science (Hume & Berry, 2011). Fazio et al. (2010) reported that preservice teachers are prepared during university coursework to engage in inquiry-based science methods and even show evidence of understanding and competence. However, during field experiences, a large number of preservice teachers fail to observe experienced teachers engaging in inquiry-based practices or be mentored in them.

Finally, in the discipline of physical education (PE), researchers have identified evidence of effective practices such as meaningful engagement but have also documented the challenge of implementing these practices in their courses. PE teacher educators find it particularly challenging to provide preservice teachers with field experiences that allow them to engage in, identify, adapt, and interpret these principles and practices (Fletcher et al., 2018). Guidance in responding to this ongoing tension between university coursework and field experiences might be provided by studies that explored teacher educator knowledge about how to respond to this issue.

Research in teacher education has not answered these questions in ways that could help resolve these tensions. While the divide is often studied, efforts to uncover teacher educator knowledge about bridging this divide have not been extensively explored. Indeed, research like Martin's (2017) study (as well as Thomas (2017) and Bullock (2017) in the same issue) that focus on what teacher educators know and understand about most effectively connecting university coursework and field experiences could guide teacher educator practice.

The tension of university coursework and field experiences extends into online teacher education as well. The trend for online teacher education has been growing alongside the general trend for more online offerings in higher education. Allen and Seaman (2013), in *Changing Course: 10 Years of Tracking Online Education in the United States,* reported that 85% of higher education institutions offered courses online, and 65% had entire programs online. Of particular concern for teacher educators is that the move to increasing numbers of online course offerings exacerbates the problem of linking university coursework and field experiences. It is challenging for teacher educators who are in online settings to model and engage their preservice teachers in evidence-based practices. Adding to the complexity for teacher educators teaching online is the task of preparing these teachers to teach in blended or online settings (Dyment & Downing, 2020; Kennedy & Archambault, 2012).

Many of the same challenges that have been documented in face-to-face teacher education are also of concern in online settings. For example, there is the same concern among various disciplines that exists in teacher education that coursework will be delivered like a textbook, rather than modeled by instructors and engaged in by students. Researchers and designers are studying innovative ways to address this concern. In science education, for example, advances have been made in teaching problem-based learning strategies online (Sulisworo & Santyasa, 2018). Just as in their face-to-face courses, online teacher educators of multicultural education still encounter reluctance from preservice teachers to shift their worldviews and integrate new knowledge about diversity. Yet online teacher educators are documenting useful and promising ways to engage preservice and in-service teachers online in transformative thinking and capture that thinking using online modalities (Grant et al., 2018).

Online teacher education in field experiences also presents both possibilities and limitations to preservice teacher learning and reveals the same tension between theory and practice. Ball and Forzani (2009) proposed the benefits of virtual environments for preservice teachers to practice targeted tasks and activities before working in real-school settings. They further suggested that digital environments could allow preservice teachers to practice some skills of teaching in designed settings, simulating a practice teaching experience that students could engage in online. There are other ways teacher educators have studied digital affordances, although most are targeted at management or developing target skills, lacking the holistic context preservice teachers face in actual field experience.

TEACHER EDUCATOR KNOWLEDGE

Given the current focus in many disciplines on teacher knowledge and related thinking, it is surprising that there is so little in the research literature on the knowledge of those who prepare teachers. Teacher educator knowledge is a developing field, as evidenced by a broad search using the Education Resources Information Center (ERIC) database and these terms: teacher educator knowledge, teacher educator AND personal practical knowledge, and teacher educator AND knowledge. A scan of these studies revealed that the attention of teacher educator knowledge has focused more in identifying types of knowledge teacher educators hold and how they may overlap, including content knowledge, pedagogical knowledge, the overlapping pedagogical content knowledge, and more recently, knowledge of technology and teaching with technology. A scan of these studies showed that within disciplines, there has been much study of pedagogical content knowledge and implications for teacher education and teacher educators (see Berry et al., 2016), but ultimately, this searching resulted in few studies that explore what teacher educator knowledge is, and how it is conceptualized.

The research into teacher knowledge – as opposed to teacher educator knowledge – is more prolific. In this section, I focus on two important perspectives on teacher knowledge, one emerging from the work of Connelly et al. (1997) on personal practical knowledge and another emerging from the work of Shulman (1986). Study of teacher knowledge surged in the 80s and 90s (Connelly et al., 1997) yet since then has not led to a robust research investigation into teacher educator knowledge. This is significant given the assumption, in a standards-based environment, that the quality of teacher education is related to teacher quality (Vanassche & Berry, 2020) and a hope that teacher educator knowledge can influence, improve, or transform teacher knowledge. In fact, the topic of teacher educator knowledge is not included in the most current *Sage Handbook of Research on Teacher Education* (Clandinin & Husu, 2017). In Loughran and Hamilton's (2016) *International Handbook of Teacher Education*, there are chapters on pedagogical content knowledge, pedagogy, pedagogical reasoning, and subject matter knowledge of teacher educators but not teacher educator knowledge. As I looked at the research I did find, I gathered those that are most relevant to what I am trying to uncover, especially Vanassche and Berry's (2020) recent chapter, Teacher Educator Knowledge, Practice, and S-STTEP Research.

I begin in *Conceptions of Teacher Knowledge* with a framing discussion of what we do know. Since teacher educator knowledge is often seen as an outgrowth of teacher knowledge, I begin by describing two major conceptions of teacher knowledge. Then, in *How Teacher Knowledge Informs Teacher Educator Knowledge*, I provide an explanation about how teacher educator knowledge does not exist comfortably alongside research on teacher knowledge and highlight tensions that exist. Next, in *Conceptions of Teacher Educator Knowledge*, I discuss characteristics of teacher educator knowledge. Finally, in *Teacher Educator Knowledge Online*, I extend the discussion to recent research on how teacher educators are using what they know to prepare teachers online and postpandemic.

Conceptions of Teacher Knowledge

Connelly and Clandinin's (1988) notion of the personal practical knowledge of teachers is particularly useful to my conception of teacher educator knowledge. By their definition, personal practical knowledge is a narrative approach to articulating how a teacher participates in educational contexts and encompasses that teacher's beliefs, practical principles, past experiences, and thinking. Connelly et al. (1997) further explained:

> Traditionally, it was assumed that teacher characteristics (e.g., warmth, firmness, punctuality) and teaching/learning methods and processes (e.g., lecture, laboratory, seat work, drill) were the main teaching areas of importance to student learning. In contrast to the concern for teacher characteristics and teaching/learning methods, the assumption in teacher knowledge research is that the most important area is what teachers know and how their knowing is expressed in teaching. On this assumption, teacher knowledge and knowing affects every aspect of the teaching act. (p. 666)

According to Connelly and Clandinin (1988), through the use of various field texts, a teacher's personal practical knowledge is conceptualized through a narrative methodology wherein the field texts are constructed as stories and analyzed to reveal a teacher's personal metaphor, philosophy, and knowledge. By considering the implications of personal practical knowledge in relation to teacher educator knowledge, teacher educators, like teachers, are also developing a language of practice in order to describe ways of being physically present in a classroom or techniques for managing groups and engaging students in learning. Certainly, teacher educators' prior experiences inform their curriculum-making and pedagogical decisions as they prepare teachers, but in the new context of teaching as a teacher educator, they may develop new, changed, or different practices.

Clandinin's (2000) explanation of teacher knowledge may also further help inform a conception of teacher educator knowledge. In this article, she referred to *knowledge for teaching* as a how-to-teach approach of a list of skills often seen in teacher education programs and proposed an alternative conceptualization called *teacher knowledge*. This alternate, more personal view is that teachers "hold knowledge that comes from experience, is learned in context, and is expressed in practice" (Clandinin, 2000, p. 30). In this way, teacher knowledge is different from knowledge for teachers, which can be normalized, standardized, and asserted (Berry et al., 2016). Arguably, this continuum ranging from the general to the situated may hold true for teacher educators as well.

A contrasting view of the knowledge teachers hold has emerged from Shulman (1986). Included in Shulman's theoretical framework is the concept of pedagogical content knowledge (PCK), which delineates a particular kind of knowledge teachers use: an amalgam of subject matter knowledge, knowledge of learners, general pedagogical knowledge, and curricular knowledge that all overlaps and informs the teacher in transforming subject matter into student learning. This concept has been expanded to include knowledge of technology, teaching technology, and using technology to teach (Koehler & Mishra, 2009; Niess, 2011).

Since Shulman's (1986) original conceptual framework was published, many in the disciplines of science, math, and technology education have built tools and assessments that attempt to measure the content knowledge, and PCK teachers should acquire and demonstrate in their respective disciplines. For example, in mathematics education, Hill et al. (2008) incorporated multiple choice surveys and used factor analysis to try to distinguish between content and pedagogical knowledge practicing teachers hold. Depaepe et al. (2013) provided a comprehensive review of the way in which the concept of pedagogical content knowledge has taken hold in mathematics education research. More recently, PCK for teacher educators was investigated in Chick and Beswick's (2018) study of a framework for identifying the PCK required by math teacher educators in order to teach preservice teachers the PCK needed for teaching mathematics. In science and other disciplines, the same kinds of surveys, advanced statistical analyses, and other quantitative methods have been employed to try to tease apart the detailed knowledge components in each of these disciplines (de Kramer et al., 2012; Loughran et al., 2012).

Indeed, Shulman's conceptual framework inspired many studies attempting to capture the knowledge and growth of teacher's pedagogical reasoning, as well as establish what exactly is a knowledge base for the various disciplines. Grossman and Shulman (1994) stated that "the different domains of teacher knowledge are inevitably interactive and interdependent," situated, complex, and not static (p. 9). Despite this assertion, this research path has often led researchers to choose methods of study and to interpret data in ways that categorize knowledge in decontextualized ways and describe findings using acquisition-oriented language, such as the building of a knowledge base (see p. 7 for Grossman and Shulman's assertion that this metaphor has been misrepresented). While it is certainly important for teachers to acquire knowledge of teaching, including subject matter expertise, general pedagogical strategies, and specific pedagogical content knowledge, this research focus has lent more support to current efforts to mandate and measure best practices and standards of teaching and less to capturing or describing the contextualized, ongoing development of types of teacher knowledge that Grossman and Shulman claim as the original purpose. This is perhaps part of the mischief of best practices referred to by Bullough (2019).

How Teacher Knowledge Research Informs Teacher Educator Knowledge

The research into teacher knowledge, in its various research paths, has helped inform teacher educators as they prepare teachers. This model is useful for positioning preservice teachers as knowers already and challenging teacher educators to enact the theories and practices they preach. Because teacher educators teach teachers, some researchers use the concepts that guided the development of the research conversation on teacher knowledge as their basis for exploring teacher educator knowledge. Yet, the two do not live very comfortably together, and it is not always clear how they fit together.

One way that teacher educator knowledge is more complex to conceptualize than teacher knowledge lies in the moral obligations that are tied to teaching teachers. If teaching is both broader and more personal than just bits of content knowledge and pedagogical skills, then one role of teacher educators may be to help preservice teachers develop their teacher knowledge. Indeed, Clandinin (2000) asserted the importance of supporting preservice teachers in recognizing what they already know and how they can draw it forward in their teaching. Using the lens of teacher knowledge based in Clandinin (2000), the job of a teacher educator is not transferring their knowledge but designing curriculum to help preservice teachers shape and reshape knowledge they already have. And while doing this, teacher educators are always keeping in mind the obligations they have not just to preservice teachers but to unseen children (Arizona Group, 1997).

A moral struggle to "walk the talk" was described by the Arizona Group as beginning teacher educators committed to learning their potential for influence within their institutions of education. Dewey (1929/2013) cautioned against the "remoteness" and disconnect that can occur between practical experience in the teaching field and research work (p. 43). (This disconnect is an echo of the tension between field experience and university coursework explored earlier in this literature review.) In a response to the tensions between traditional and progressive approaches to education, Dewey (1938/2007) asserted that no matter the approach, students should have freedom to seek and make connections and that teachers have a task to design meaningful, connected learning experiences that students may choose to engage in. For Dewey, it was important for teachers to be constantly interrogating both learning and practice and taking into account the personal experience and education of the learner. Thus, curriculum should be carefully chosen and activities designed for educative moments to occur. The experiences of teachers, informed by and informing their own understandings of content and pedagogy, are also crucial to their craft. While teachers design such learning experiences for students, teacher educators are concerned about creating curricula that will result in teachers (preservice and in-service) developing educative learning experiences for their students.

This description of teacher knowledge as situated in curriculum, informed by the teacher's experience, and in connection to the learner also informs a conception of teacher educator knowledge (Connelly & Clandinin, 1988). Just as with teacher knowledge, teacher educator knowledge is potentially entwined with personal experience and theory, yet teacher educators often do their work of preparing teachers in remote or disruptive contexts, unseen and not seeing, disconnected from their students, schools, and even from their research.

Another area of complexity is that while many teacher educators first gained their experience as teachers, it is not to be assumed that a good teacher inevitably becomes a good teacher educator (Hadar & Brody, 2017). When they begin work in higher education, teacher educators bring with them their experiences with prior K-12 students, the knowledge of their discipline, be it PE or history, and the contextual experience they have gained in teaching their discipline to children. They continue to draw from the knowledge they gain from research they have conducted and any other experience that has informed their work of preparing preservice teachers. However, teacher education involves a new context (higher institution), new (adult) students, new obligations (research, field supervision, etc.), and therefore new ways of thinking about teaching and learning. Indeed, there is evidence that teacher educators do use teacher knowledge acquired prior to teaching at colleges of education but with a different focus (Arizona Group, 1995). Teacher knowledge focuses on how to engage students in learning the content, whereas teacher educator knowledge focuses of course on helping preservice teachers gain particular knowledge, but part of that knowledge that makes teacher educator knowledge unique is how to support preservice teachers in developing teacher knowledge that will allow them to design curriculum and activities that their future students can learn from. There is further evidence that teacher educators must teach in even more layered, complex, and personally vulnerable ways than teachers (e.g., Pinnegar, Hutchinson, & Hamilton, 2020; Whiting & Cutri, 2015).

The complexity of defining teacher educator knowledge is further compounded by the variety of backgrounds, disciplines, and experience of teacher educators which defy the typical. One reason why is that the path of teacher educators does not follow a straightforward academic trajectory, and teacher educators come to their understanding of teaching preservice teachers often after they are hired as teacher educators, and often after other professional careers. The widely varied professional experience and graduate education of teacher educators is even further complicated by a number of teacher education faculty who did not begin their careers as school teachers (Newberry, 2014).

Finally, being a teacher educator is different than being a teacher in part because the teaching that occurs to prepare teachers is also different. Therefore, the research into teacher educator knowledge is informed by the research of teacher knowledge but is not necessarily just a simple expansion of that. This next section will begin to make clear some of the most recent ways that teacher educator knowledge has been conceptualized and studied, especially using forms of intimate scholarship such as Self-Study of Teacher Educator Practices (S-STEP).

Conceptions of Teacher Educator Knowledge

In their recent chapter, Vanassche and Berry (2020) asserted that in trying to measure knowledge and performance of teacher educator quality, there is a risk of thinking of teacher educator knowledge as merely a list of competencies to be acquired. When teacher educators have shown evidence of their skill, there is an assumption of that knowledge as static, implying "the notion of general, context-free knowledge that can be transferred from one situation to the next … regardless of the practice setting" (p. 186). This view contrasts with a "view of teacher educator knowledge as that which manifests itself and constantly develops in and through practice" (p. 178). It is this contextualized and holistic view that recognizes teaching as fundamentally relational that I describe here. Also important in accounting for teacher educator knowledge is that the most important goal is for teacher educators to understand what they know (Fenstermacher, 1994; Vanassche & Berry, 2020). The following characteristics of teacher educator knowledge reveal the ongoing tensions of teacher education and show "the nature and shape of teacher educator knowledge as tacit, complex, often contradictory, situated, relational, and moral" (p. 181).

One characteristic of teacher educator knowledge is that it is tacit, often only made visible and understood in practice (Vanassche & Berry, 2020, p. 188). In Berry's careful data collection and analysis using Open Journals, she reveals that she may make choices without always being able to articulate why. According to Vanassche and Berry (2020):

> Implicit in Berry's excerpts is a conception of teacher educator knowledge not as "the application of scientific theory and technique to the instrumental problems of practice" (Schön, 1987, p. 30), but theoretical knowledge of her work is brought to life through her actions in practice. These actions do not appear to be governed by specific rules, nor does she have a straightforward way to determine which actions are more or less appropriate to pursue in the given circumstances. General descriptions of and for teacher educators' work, for example, in terms of standards, cannot do full justice to the complexity that characterizes this practice. (p. 189)

Because of the tacit nature of teacher educator knowledge, a perfectly reasonable response to the uncertainty that arises in the moment when making teaching decisions is, "It depends."

A second characteristic of teacher educator knowledge is that it is complex or "messy more than tidy" (p. 184). The contexts of teacher education are myriad and tension-filled, the mandates, requirements, and rules vary from place to place, theories and purposes and practices are often disparate, and these tensions are ongoing, irreconcilable, and fraught with multiple stakeholders. The tension-filled nature of teacher education and the difficulty in resolving those tensions has been made clear in this literature review. It is within these tension-filled contexts that teacher educators enact their teacher educator knowledge.

Teacher educators each have individual experiences and a unique knowledge base. Even an important skill taught long ago to me as a preservice English teacher, such as how to write a persuasive essay, becomes highly individualized knowledge when I take it up as a teacher educator who first taught adolescent students to write essays using pencil and paper at a locked-in behavioral treatment hospital, studied literacy and learning for diverse adolescent learners, then studied second language acquisition, then taught preservice teachers in Teaching English to Speakers of Other Languages (TESOL) about language and literacy for English learners, while sitting alongside my own children as they composed arguments and supporting details for their teachers using Google Docs and Utah Compose. This constellation of experiences and the knowledge that informed them becomes a part of my knowledge as a teacher educator. Thus, each teacher educator, even within the same discipline, will have a different résumé and particular wisdom about how to teach students to compose a persuasive essay, and further, how to prepare preservice teachers to do the same. Thus, teacher educator knowledge may be local but when unpacked and made explicit may inform a broader, shared understanding of "complex professional know-how, understandings, and practices" (Vanassche & Berry, 2020, p. 202). In their handbook chapter on teacher educator knowledge, Vanassche and Berry (2020) provided clear evidence of this assertion, in their case for science teacher educators.

Another characteristic of teacher educator knowledge is that it is often contradictory. Vanassche and Berry (2020) named several contradictions encountered by Berry as a teacher educator, including:

> ...the specific "tensions" of "telling and growth," "confidence and uncertainty," "planning and being responsive," "safety and challenge," "action and intent," and "valuing and reconstructing experience" that actively hold contradiction and ambiguity together in her experiencing of, and learning about, teaching. (p. 203)

One contradiction for teacher educators lies in conventional metaphors of teaching and learning, which emerge from an acquisition metaphor for learning, revealed in language and carried out in cultural norms (Sfard, 1998). In Sfard's continuum of learning, acquisition-type language is understood in terms of concepts to be accumulated, refined, combined, or built. This approach to learning aligns with economic, or banking, principles. In this context, the metaphor for learning is to gain possession over a commodity.

At the other end of the Sfard's (1998) continuum, a participation metaphor for learning includes vocabulary such as legitimate peripheral participation, dialogue, communities of inquiry or practice, context, social mediation, practice, relationship, and discourse. In a participatory context, the metaphor for learning may be movement from the edges toward the center, a process of becoming a member of a community – engaging in the language and norms of that community until full participation is reached (Lave & Wenger, 1991).

At their extremes on the continuum, an acquisition metaphor leads us to think too literally, as if knowledge is material or property, and a participatory metaphor for learning can sound promising but not be any less susceptible to abuse. Because an acquisition metaphor for learning is so common, in teaching contexts, it is difficult to avoid acquisitionist language and thinking when considering expectations for students. In teacher education, it is similarly difficult to avoid acquisitionist language, to model participatory teaching, and invite potentially resistant students to consider new conceptions of learning. These contradictions in teaching are often revealed in conceptions of teacher education knowledge, programs, and practices. While research and programs that align with a partic-ipatory learning theory are present in the research literature, the implementation and discussion of such research is often problematized by policy and cultural norms more aligned to an acquisition approach. These contradictions in learning theories and commitments to teaching preservice teachers the accompanying practices reside not just in contradictions and tensions teacher educators encounter in their own thinking, but they must navigate these contradictions within the teacher education programs in which they teach in respectful ways. This means they often must employ their knowledge of teaching and teacher education to design curricula that responds to these contradictions as they educate teachers.

Another characteristic of teacher educator knowledge is that it is situated. Situated learning is explained well by Lave and Wenger's (1991) theory of legitimate peripheral participation, a learning theory that is more participatory than acquisitional on Sfard's (1998) continuum. Teacher educator knowledge is situated in that it exists in a community, likely more than one, such as a com-munity of other teacher educators, or a partnership/cohort/class/research group of in-service teachers, preservice teachers, and teacher educators. Teacher educator knowledge in a situated sense is intrinsically connected to context, including a particular time and space, and resists being generalized. Vanassche and Berry (2020) described "teacher educator knowledge as that which is enacted in practice, while engaged in one's professional activities, as constantly evolving and developing from experience, and as situated in a particular context" (p. 188).

Teacher educator knowledge is also relational, based in an ontology that recognizes the intimate nature of such knowledge (Hamilton et al., 2016). Both the teacher educator and preservice teachers have obligations and contributions to make to the success of the learning (Kitchen, 2005). This is something that is not always well understood. Again, referring to Berry's work, Vanassche and Berry (2020) stated:

> The knowledge under study in Berry's work is thus not an individual attribute but a socio-relational accomplishment that is continuously shaped and reshaped through the actions that she takes in response to the needs of the particular practice situation in which she finds herself and the others (her student teachers and the future children in their classrooms but also teacher educator colleagues, etc.) present in that situation. (p. 184)

Like the Arizona Group's (1997) obligations to unseen children, Berry rec-ognizes the connection and commitment she has not just to her face-to-face preservice teachers but also with their students, her colleagues, and families. In this relational sense, teacher educator knowledge is also ongoing because both a teacher educator and preservice teacher can continue learning through reflection even when the class or the interaction is ended, even years later.

This leads to a last characteristic of teacher educator knowledge as moral. If there were no moral element to the work of teacher education, a technical skills approach would be the only useful conversation, but because of contexts and relationships, teacher educators do have a sense of their obligations and responsibilities within these boundaries (Bullough, 2019). In accounting for the moral nature of teacher educator knowledge Vanassche and Berry (2020) explained, "Knowledge becomes visible as practice (what we do) is studied and unpacked and includes the perceptual elements of that practice (how we feel) as well as the conceptual (how we think)" (p. 192). In this way, teacher educator knowledge emerges from and informs the tensions and constraints within the field. Pinnegar and Murphy (2019) suggest that teacher educators often label concerns as moral which are actually either ethical or moral concerns. Ethical issues are related to the personal, the close, the student in front of you, and the obligations a teacher educator has to that student. Moral issues are related to obligations a teacher educator has to the profession, community, content, and are characterized by more distance from the immediate relationships. These issues of obligations, commitments, and responsibilities have been explored in the literature review. Ethical and moral issues also guide decisions such as in-the-moment pedagogical reasoning, curriculum design, larger scopes such as program and policy design, and essentially all interactions with preservice teachers, institutions, and schools.

Teacher Educator Knowledge Online

Research in online teacher education that enlightens a conception of teacher educator knowledge as described by Vanassche and Berry (2020) is limited. Studies that explore how teacher educator knowledge that is "tacit, complex, often contradictory, situated, relational, and moral" (p. 181) represent an important beginning to uncovering teacher educator knowledge in online contexts. In one such study, Bullock and Fletcher (2017) conducted a collaborative self-study in which they investigated closely particular online practices, such as asynchronous communication with students, that challenged their own sense of teacher educator identity and led them to explore how the parameters of an online setting influenced and shaped embodied interactions. In another recent study, as online teacher educators who "privilege the role of relationship," Murphy and Pinnegar (2018) studied the syllabi and evaluations from their online courses and uncovered findings regarding the value and shifts of the relational in an online context. Cutri, Mena, and Whiting (2020) found that during the pandemic, professors in higher education at one institution showed a willingness to learn and even a hope to do well as they made the transition to online teaching. It is often in moments of transition, change, or revisiting that can cause tacit knowing to emerge and be articulated. In the current climate of prevalent online teacher education, it is important to continue such research.

PREPARING TEACHERS POSTPANDEMIC AND IN THE FUTURE

As teacher educators prepare teachers for unknown changes and challenges, they are faced with the same pressures and obligations as in the past. Their work is to move preservice teachers into engaging as practitioners. According to Schön

(1987), this means engaging them in complex thinking and reflecting about teaching and learning, increased willingness to practice strategies that build academic skills, and differentiate that instruction for all learners. In many ways, this description has not varied much over the years. Since the current shift and increase in online teacher education, it is especially important for teacher educator knowledge to be investigated in online contexts.

Especially since the onset of the COVID-19 pandemic and coming out of emergency remote teaching, the challenges facing teacher educators to prepare their students using online formats and pressure for a market-reform of teacher education are even more high profile. The United Nations Educational, Scientific and Cultural Organization (UNESCO) calls the COVID-19 pandemic the largest education disruption in history, with 90% of the world's student population out of their classrooms for a time, only heightening inequitable learning opportunities worldwide (UNESCO, 2020).

A further complication is that teacher educators are not only required to develop knowledge and pedagogical skill for teaching in online formats but increasingly they are required to prepare preservice teachers, within their regular teacher education courses, to teach both in person and online. Of particular concern is educating teachers to employ digital and pedagogical skills that promote inquiry-based practices that research has shown to be most effective. This is exacerbated by the need for teacher educators to embrace and promote issues of equity and social justice. Such work requires teacher educators to engage teachers in ways that will shift their thinking and their practice. Some, such as Cutri, Whiting, and Bybee (2020), have conducted work exploring the potential of online education to support preservice teachers in engaging in critical pedagogy in both thinking and action. Yet, as online teacher education pervades the world, the many demands made of teacher educators seem only to grow.

In this environment of increased online teacher education and as we are emerging out of emergency remote teaching, teacher educators still operate within the ongoing tension of enacting teacher education within institutions of higher education, the tension of teacher preparation as training or education, and the tension of the value of university coursework versus field experience. As discussed in this literature review, these tensions of teacher education are fully engaged and even heightened by the changes and considerations that emerge in the implementation of online teacher education. By studying teacher educators' knowledge as they shift from teaching in-person to online, the research community could benefit from careful accounts of this knowledge. Indeed, studies that investigate those teacher education practices and knowledge particularly attuned to changing teacher belief and disposition, as well as document how these practices and knowledge may be enacted and effective in online settings, would be important for supporting teacher educators as they engage in curriculum making for online teacher education.

WHAT METHODOLOGY AND ACCOMPANYING STRATEGIES ALLOW US TO UNCOVER TEACHER EDUCATOR KNOWLEDGE?

ABSTRACT

In this chapter, the details of the design chosen to uncover teacher educator knowledge for this study are explained. By choosing Self-Study of Teacher Education Practices (S-STEP), this methodology positions researchers to examine their own practice and explore beliefs and moral and political values, thereby adding to the research conversation of teacher education, and also turn what we learn into improvement of practice. Self-study of practice is a methodology but without a proscribed set of methods. Rather, other methods of qualitative analysis are employed in self-study. A variety of qualitative methods such as dialogue, a critical friend, exemplars, and analytic narrative vignettes were selected and implemented in order to collect, organize, analyze, and present the data. Issues of positionality and ethics are also addressed. This chapter ends with a discussion about trustworthiness and rigor in relation to methodological approaches and strategies employed in qualitative research, especially highlighting the inherent vulnerable nature of self-study research, and the importance of protecting participants and researchers.

Keywords: Self-study of practice; qualitative methodologies; analytic narrative vignettes; exemplars; dialogue; critical friendship; trustworthiness; moral dimensions of teaching; tacit knowledge; teacher educator knowledge

At the onset of the COVID-19 pandemic in North America, many classes in higher education were rushed to online formats. Without much time for teachers to transition and prepare, these courses were in most cases modified versions of in-person iterations of the courses. Indeed, these online courses seldom followed research-based practices for engaging learners and supporting all learners online. In the news and on blogs, this phenomenon has been described as "paddling a life raft" (Vergroesen, 2020). It was in the context of these emergency educational responses in the spring of 2020, that this research was conducted.

Exploring Teacher Educator Knowledge
Advances in Research on Teaching, Volume 48, 35–49
Copyright © 2025 Celina Dulude Lay
Published under exclusive licence by Emerald Publishing Limited
ISSN: 1479-3687/doi:10.1108/S1479-368720240000048003

By examining my own teacher educator knowledge during a time of transition, I hoped to make a useful contribution to the research conversation in teacher education by identifying strands of teacher educator knowledge that were implicit or tacit in my teaching. This chapter reports the details of the design of this narrative self-study which addressed the primary research wonder about what I knew as a teacher educator. What constituted my tacit and embodied teacher educator knowledge that became visible as I redesigned an in person course to be taught online? By outlining the theoretical approaches and justifications for the research design, each procedure and strategy can then be examined for its particular usefulness as a research tool.

First, I articulate the theoretical approaches and modes of inquiry that were the foundation for the research design. Then I outline the procedures of the study, including setting, participants, data collection procedures, and analysis. Within each of these sections, I include rationales for my choice of methodology. Finally, I conclude with a description and reiteration of the strategies used throughout the study to establish trustworthiness.

DESIGN

This study was founded in Self-Study of Teacher Education Practices (S-STEP) and drew on a variety of qualitative methods such as dialogue, a critical friend, exemplars, and analytic narrative vignettes in order to collect, organize, analyze, and present the data.

Self-Study of Teacher Education Practices

I approached my research question as a wonder about my own transition to online teaching and what and how it revealed my teacher educator knowledge, not the personal accumulation of teaching competencies, but rather a contextualized, holistic, and relational application of what I know as a teacher educator. Since I was focusing on my understanding and knowledge within my own practice as a teacher educator, S-STEP was an appropriate choice for this study of teacher educator knowledge, particularly since shifting to online instruction made that knowledge visible as I designed, taught and reflected on my teaching. Regarding the study of one's own practice as a teacher educator, LaBoskey (2004) noted that "we feel responsible for the immediate implementation of any new understandings that result from our research," and S-STEP research "needs to extend beyond the epistemological into learning theory, beliefs about the nature of teaching, and moral, ethical, and political values regarding the means and ends of education" (p. 818). The purposes and characteristics of this study aligned with LaBoskey's (2004) assertions about S-STEP. Since teacher educator knowledge is an emerging field and most research findings concerning it have been captured through S-STEP inquiries (Vanassche & Berry, 2020), this was the methodology used in this study.

EXPLORING TEACHER EDUCATOR KNOWLEDGE

In 2005, Zeichner echoed an earlier call by Ducharme and Ducharme (1996) for educational researchers to conduct more studies on teacher educators themselves. He broadened this call to include teacher education curricula, instructional practices, and the question of whether it matters if the courses taught take place in a school, university campus, in person or online. Since then, other than S-STEP, there have been few studies that have added to the research focused on what we know about teacher educators and what they know about their own professional knowledge (Berry, 2007; Pinnegar, Lay, et al., 2020). Additionally, there is a distinct lack of studies that articulate knowledge specific to teacher educators, and not much at all about teacher educator knowledge that emerges in online settings.

This study was established within a teacher educator working partnership of two co-teacher educators collaborating as researcher (myself) and critical friend (Dr Pinnegar) (Pinnegar & Hamilton, 2009). According to LaBoskey (2004), the five characteristics of S-STEP are that it is self-initiated and focused, improvement-aimed, interactive, includes multiple, mainly qualitative methods, and it defines validity as a validation process based in trustworthiness (p. 817). This research met these characteristics of S-STEP because I, the researcher, studied my own practice as a teacher educator preparing for and teaching a course online that I had previously taught in-person. I collected data on my own thinking, progress, and understandings. As I undertook this project, I understood interrogation of the data using an interactive method of dialogue and working with a critical friend would be the strongest way to uncover my thinking on the decisions I made in design, teaching, and assessing. My teacher educator knowledge was embedded in the strategies and techniques I employed in the course. Analyzing these using dialogue and interaction with a critical friend enabled me to uncover the knowledge embedded the design decisions I made (Pinnegar & Hamilton, 2009).

This project is a clear example of self-study because it exhibits the characteristics noted by LaBoskey (2004). I, the main researcher, initiated the project, and a part of the focus was on my own learning. This study was improvement-aimed because I considered my own teacher educator knowledge while constructing online curriculum for preservice teachers in order to improve the quality of education and teaching in both spheres. The study was collaborative because it was contextualized in a working partnership of researcher and critical friend (Schuck & Russell, 2005) where I redesigned a course I had already taught in person as an online course for preservice teachers. My assumption was that much of my teacher educator knowledge is embodied and tacit. When we design a course, we are constantly in a decision-making mode. Our tacit and embodied knowledge guides us; therefore, as we interrogate and examine those decisions, our knowledge becomes visible. Indeed, our teacher knowledge became visible as I and my critical friend shifted from teaching in one format (in-person) to teaching in another (online).

S-STEP research is a methodology, but it does not, like many other methodologies, have proscribed methods. As a result, it is common for S-STEP researchers to employ methods, strategies, and techniques from other methodologies in collecting and analyzing data (Pinnegar & Hamilton, 2009). In this study, I drew on such qualitative methods as critical friendship, dialogue, and analytic narrative vignettes. Critical friendship and dialogue are explained further here. In the next chapter, the elements and process of constructing and interpreting analytic narrative vignettes will be articulated.

Critical Friendship

A critical friend is someone who is knowledgeable about qualitative research methodologies and skilled at interpreting data in relationship to already existing research and theory. The critical friend is critical in terms of approaching data interpretation as analysis rather than critique. Their role is to question the interpretation of the researcher and push the researcher to provide evidence to support the interpretation. Thus, the involvement of a critical friend is a technique in qualitative research to aid in interpretation of findings and improve trustworthiness of a study. By inviting a critical friend, the researcher is more likely to see interpretations in ways not always thought of by one researcher alone (Hamilton & Pinnegar, 2015).

Another component of employing a critical friend is that it tends to create a research action loop, meaning that as I prepared, engaged in dialogue, taught, and engaged in more dialogue with a critical friend, a relational space for interrogating the research question was built. Critical friendship is a focused, personal, research-informed practice that yielded a rich learning environment for identifying teacher educator knowledge and for discovering ways to improve practice even during phases of data collection and in the midst of course teaching. The critical friend played a vital role in questioning, deepening interpretation, and pointing to details in the data that might otherwise have been overlooked.

Dialogue in S-STEP

Just like the scientific method in quantitative research is a tool for securing knowledge, dialogue is a similar tool in qualitative research, particularly self-study of practice research. Dialogue enables researchers to interrogate, interpret, and establish trustworthy findings in qualitative forms of research. As a tool for coming to know, it is a collaborative analysis technique that can reveal multiple ways of understanding data and arriving at meaningful interpretation. According to Hamilton and Pinnegar (2015):

> Within dialogue, ideas are put forth, shaped, transformed, rejected, embraced, or secured. Within dialogue ideas are always strengthened and expanded. The intimate scholar through engagement with dialogue negotiates the meaning of and evidence for the interpretation formed.... Intimate scholars intentionally seek out variability of opinion and submit their thinking to critique and response. Thus, understanding emerges through discussion and careful consideration.... It is through submission to a process of dialogue that the value and verity of the scholars' own interpretation gains strength and the inquirer develops confidence in what he or she has come to understand concerning his study. (p. 190)

As described, the process of dialogue was useful and relevant for this study because it enabled me to explore more complexly and completely the tacit and embodied knowledge that lay under the decisions I was making. Thus, it enabled me to make visible the knowledge implicit and hidden in my data and decision-making. I defined teacher educator knowledge using Vanassche and Berry's (2020) holistic definition, characterized as "tacit, complex, often contradictory, situated, relational, and moral" (p. 181). Therefore, dialogue as a research tool was an appropriate choice for expanding understanding and negotiating meanings of teacher educator knowledge in terms of being tacit, complex, complicated, situated, relational, and moral.

Analytic Narrative Vignettes

An analytic narrative vignette is a compilation of significant bits and pieces from the numerous narrative accounts that provides a comprehensive narrative for a particular thematic unit. Narrative vignettes are constructed using multiple stories and many pieces of the data as a whole. It might be comprised of a single story with added details from additional stories, or it might be a plotline based on the theme filled out using other details and narrative from the data. The composition of analytic narrative vignettes is an especially useful technique when a researcher is faced with an overwhelming amount of data and citing multiple instances of the theme rather than a comprehensive representation is problematic and unwieldy.

In this study, I wrote three analytic narrative vignettes, each of which contain within them representative exemplars of events, conversations, and ongoing analysis that occurred during planning, teaching, and reflecting. By carefully considering the recorded Zoom meetings, written notes, artifacts of the course, and composing them into a vignette, I was able to sift through key events, notice significant patterns or themes, and begin to make analytic choices explicit.

PROCEDURES

In S-STEP, since the researcher is also the researched, it was important for methods to be transparent and steps clearly outlined. The next sections explain this process, including a description of setting, positionality, participants, ethics, and data collection. Then I give a description of analysis, including an explanation of turning field notes into analytic narrative vignettes and how they were used for analysis and representation of findings. I end with a discussion of trustworthiness and rigor, although within each section of this chapter I have also explained how I attended to issues of trustworthiness and rigor.

Setting

In contrast to the rushed and drastic emergency remote teaching reported by Vergroesen (2020) and others, Stefinee Pinnegar and I had already made one of the courses in the Teaching English Language Learners (TELL) program into an online course, and we had already begun work on transitioning this course on content and language integration (TELL 440) to an online format. The course was conducted for 10 sessions, meeting twice a week for five weeks during BYU's spring term of 2020. All in-person classes at BYU had shifted online for the end of the winter semester, and for this new term, TELL 440 was conducted entirely from a distance using Zoom meetings. Fourteen students, all elementary education majors, signed up for the course, one of the last classes required before a final practicum field experience in schools with English learners.

Students were already familiar with concepts from previous courses such as multicultural education, principles of second language acquisition, inclusive pedagogy, and literacy instruction. In this course, students are required to apply their prior knowledge about English learners and develop new knowledge focused on how to make content comprehensible to English learners within regular classrooms and regular course instruction. Each session met for two and a half hours, and when the course was in person, students met together in groups of four or five to work on the final curriculum project. Since the course was predominantly project-based, for this online version, we decided to increase the project-based focus of the course. This meant that preservice teachers would work in small groups in breakout rooms for at least the last hour of each session.

Typically, students of this course are elementary education undergraduate students between the ages of 20 and 25, in the latter years of their university degree, just preparing for a practicum field experience working with English learners in schools. While most were elementary education majors, some may have had additional minors in special education or early childhood education. According to university policy, the spring term students at BYU met for classes online and for the most part participated in class from their permanent home addresses. Most states had implemented a strategy of shelter in place in response to the COVID-19 pandemic.

The TELL 440 course, Integrating Content and Language Instruction, is one both Stefinee Pinnegar and I had taught many times over the past decade in classroom settings. While I have only taught the course to preservice teachers, the courses, as originally designed, were meant to be delivered as distance professional development resulting in a Teaching English to Speakers of Other Languages (TESOL) endorsement for practicing teachers. Stefinee Pinnegar was involved at the conception of the TELL program to author the program design, to make wise decisions about the content to be included and the activities that would be enacted so that students could learn that content, and later to direct the program's implementation. Initially, the courses were taught on-site by a partnering school district's own teachers, trained by BYU instructors to facilitate. Each 10-session course was designed to build to the next course, hold teachers accountable for the content they had already learned, and engage in projects that were present in their practice. The courses would culminate in a TESOL endorsement for in-service teachers who participated in all six courses.

The course was online but built on knowledge and pedagogy from the in-person teaching as part of a spiral curriculum where techniques taught in previous courses were revisited and understandings deepened. An underlying theme in this course development is enabling teachers to change their thinking and promote success for students. The purpose of the course is to support teachers seeking to learn how to promote the language and literacy development of English learners. This course in particular is typically a challenging course where students bring together what they have learned about second language acquisition, multicultural education, assessment for diverse learners, and literacy in order to design a unit of activity centers that integrates content with language and literacy development as a part of general classroom instruction. As a result, both the original design, including assignments, rubrics, and assignments, and the shift in those elements to an online context was a rich site for uncovering my teacher educator knowledge.

In some forms of research, a description of setting is kept very neutral so that empirical findings may be generalized to other settings. However, this study employed S-STEP methodology, which is grounded in intimate scholarship and oriented to studies of the particular. Such studies are structured to enable readers to determine the applicability of findings to their own settings and research. Therefore, while there is often not enough space to provide all the details of the setting, it is important that researchers identify and provide the relevant details that would allow research findings to be applied and allow others to do similar studies. In addition, the orientation of these studies is toward ontology rather than abstractionist epistemology (Slife, 2004). The study seeks to account for what is rather than make truth claims based in a modernist epistemology. Further, similar to other intimate scholarship, this study has the characteristics of particularity, vulnerability, and openness; therefore, providing a description of the characteristics and making all features of the setting visible is fundamental. The findings of this study are not meant to be generalizable but to provide an honest accounting of a particular experience in a particular place and time. Putnam (2004) argues the necessity for educational research to attend more carefully to the particular in order to develop research that will be more likely to provide powerful, innovative, and essential findings for education and other social science.

Therefore, it is important to point out that in this context, the researcher is vulnerable because it was impossible to hide the setting. In addition, since I worked with a critical friend, Stefinee Pinnegar, I felt a heightened responsibility to work ethically with both of us in our accounting, descriptions, and record-keeping. Because our setting and research method demanded openness and included interpretation that is ongoing (never completely shut down), it positioned me as a researcher as always subject to uncertainty. Again, while I took careful caution to maintain confidentiality of students or other colleagues, my own interpretations and attempts to establish trustworthiness were and always will be vulnerable.

Researcher Positionality

One of the stated goals of S-STEP is to turn the research both inward and outward. The researcher should use the findings to improve their own practice and are obligated to connect the findings to the wider conversation in teacher education. I began very personally, however, by choosing a few words to position myself in the study. I do not believe that I or others emerged with fixed uniform identities or outcomes from my study nor was that ever intended. As Pinnegar, Hutchinson, and Hamilton (2020) emphasized in their handbook chapter on S-STEP, I believe in multiplicity of perspectives and openness. Based on the experience and understanding of the reader, findings are open to interpretation and re-interpretation and thus never closed and final. The context of this study is that it was a study of myself and my practice in designing an online version of a course I had previously taught in person. I also recognize that the context and my reflection on it was not static because of the movement from my past work in designing this course for an in-person format contrasted against my thinking in designing and implementing the course in an online format.

In writing the methodology section of this chapter, I have been careful to articulate the design of the study and the processes involved in data collection and analysis. As the researcher and researched, I engaged in the process of dialogue from the very beginning of data collection, data analysis and interpretation, and even into the representation of findings and construction of a conclusion. Because dialogue, a critical friend, and analysis of analytic narrative vignettes were involved in my approach for coming to know, reflexivity is a central feature of this study. Throughout the process, I was self-critical and engaged self-consciously in reflection and analysis. As I conducted this study, I was critically aware of the ways in which my teacher educator knowledge connected to race, class, and gender, influenced my thinking, and shaped my experiences.

Participants

This study was not a collaborative S-STEP. Rather, I was the main participant in this S-STEP, and I conducted the study in relationship to a critical friend, Dr Stefinee Pinnegar. In this critical friendship, her role was to assist me in examining my teaching practice and teacher educator knowledge using a process of dialogue, and especially by providing a critique of the data and an alternate lens through which to examine my analysis and findings. While much of the designing of the course and implementation of our curriculum occurred together, as the inquirer, I was the one collecting data on both our deliberation and reflections of what we were thinking, as well as our presentation to students. Since I conducted research during the preparation and teaching of an online course, I also had instructor access to Zoom recordings, student responses, interactions, and assignments. According to the parameters of my Internal Review Board approval, I did not use students as participants. Students appeared in the data for the most part collectively and through our reflection on specific experiences with them or our predictions about how students might respond. Since I never referred to students by name in the field notes, their information was kept confidential. In this study, even though I was working alongside students, I was focused on my pedagogy and my thinking about it. Both Stefinee Pinnegar and I were aware of and committed to protecting the identity of those preservice teachers in our class; therefore, we did not refer to them by name or directly quote them.

EXPLORING TEACHER EDUCATOR KNOWLEDGE

Ethics is one of the critical issues in S-STEP work. Since the researcher and the researched are the same person, it is impossible to keep their own identity private, and sometimes because they are recognizable, researchers must take extra care in protecting the identity of students, other teachers or teacher educators, and colleagues (Pinnegar & Murphy, 2019). Ethics is indeed a major concern for all S-STEP researchers in any study in which they engage, and I took responsibility to act ethically in this research project.

Another ethical consideration, since in S-STEP the researcher is also the researched, is to oneself. In this way, as I met with Dr Pinnegar to prepare curriculum, examine our decisions, and discuss together our findings, we as researchers attempted to be forthright rather than sentimental in our accounting. I recognized the importance of representing ourselves honestly, and we attempted to maintain that balance without oversharing.

Ethics Approval

This research was approved by Brigham Young University's Internal Review Board. By gaining approval, I am making transparent the ways that students in the course were protected both during the teaching and in the research design. Also, I could explain that I, along with Stefinee Pinnegar as a critical friend, entered this research fully aware of our obligations as researchers and of the personal vulnerability of this method of data collection and analysis.

In addition, I asked for and received a waiver for informed consent because this is an S-STEP. Therefore, in designing the study, I informed myself of the nuances of the study, and both I and my critical friend were aware of any risk to us. One of the risks in S-STEP is that if we are really honest about who we are, what we are thinking, and what we have done, people may be critical, dismissive, or antagonistic as a result. In such work, our own status as researchers and teacher educators becomes vulnerable.

We were especially attuned to the risk to the students in our course because of research we had done with our own children (Pinnegar et al., 2005). Because our children were young, we used their real names as we told stories about them that ended up in our final document. As they have grown, we realized what a mistake that was because it had the potential to put our relationship with them at risk and represent them in ways they would not appreciate as they grew older. Since then, we've approached our children after they became adults and they were not concerned.

Regarding the undergraduates who were enrolled in the course or who worked as teaching assistants, we were very careful to, as much as possible, maintain their anonymity. I have removed any identifiers and composed exemplars within analytic narrative vignettes that further anonymize real student information from the final representations of data in the analysis. I was concerned about the need to protect the anonymity of the students enrolled in the course; however, since I did not use student work, conduct interviews, or record observations of students, the main concern for confidentiality and informed consent pertained most clearly to

44   *What Allows Us to Uncover Teacher Educator knowledge?*

me and my critical friend. Both of us have conducted this kind of work in the past, and therefore, we fully understood the risks.

Data Collection

As researchers determine their data collection processes, they need to be constantly aware of whether an analysis of the data they collect will be able to answer the question they have posed. Since this was a study of my own practice, the data included accounts of my curriculum making and analysis of this process. This included descriptions of the work of preparing and enacting the course and my examination of the curriculum design, records of thinking about design, and analysis of the activities and decisions as constructed and enacted. It also included my reflections about our experiences before, during, and after teaching. As a result, I will describe data collection as occurring in three phases: Planning, Teaching, and Reflecting.

Specifically, I created a decision trail which included how I and my critical friend designed class activities, made decisions about pedagogy, and adjusted any rubrics or assignments already in place from the in-person course. Before teaching, these data began with our planning and included the articulation of the pedagogy and our theoretical orientations concerning teaching and learning. While teaching, data were gathered on the implementation of the curriculum and also included any adjustments and field notes about what I uncovered about my practice and my teacher educator knowledge. Also, while teaching, I recorded extensive field notes, including email correspondence, dialogue with my critical friend, and personal journaling. After teaching, data collection continued when I constructed my interpretations of the data into analytic narrative vignettes and met with my critical friend to engage in dialogue as a tool to interrogate and deepen understandings of the data. In this stage, I built on that process by drawing into the data collection journaling, emails, and artifacts from the course that were related to planning, teaching, and reflecting.

While it may appear that I collected everything, I did not. I carefully targeted data that would enable me to uncover my teacher educator knowledge in terms of my decision-making, my action, and reflection during the course. This enabled me to make visible teacher educator knowledge that was essentially embedded and embodied in my action and tacit in terms of my thinking.

Before Teaching. Before teaching, I and my critical friend developed the content, which involved discussions of overarching goals and working sessions to move class activities and assignments from an in-person format to online. This included constructing a syllabus, course outline, new course activities, and publishing the course. As part of this process, I articulated my commitments in terms of engaging the students in supporting their learning.

The demands of using dialogue as a process of coming to know meant that data collection and interpretation of data was ongoing in order to more completely attend to the teacher educator knowledge that emerged and the shift in my thinking about pedagogy online in juxtaposition with an in-person format. In planning, I had multiple conversations with Stefinee Pinnegar who was also a

EXPLORING TEACHER EDUCATOR KNOWLEDGE 45

co-instructor for the course. These conversations were often spur-of-the moment; therefore, rather than tape recording, I instead used a method of constructing field texts outlined by Clandinin and Connelly (2000). As part of my field texts, I constructed written field notes of our conversations during our planning meetings for the course. These field notes were based on notes taken in preparing for and teaching the course and included journaling, emails, notes from meetings, and development of artifacts such as assignments, rubrics, and other course documents. Also included were field texts that reported our reflections about teacher educator knowledge identified in the moment of our discussions and thinking about planning or subsequent reflections on planning.

During Teaching. Once the course began, I added as a source of data collection field notes of the discussions that took place before class, the debriefing conversations that occurred after teaching each class, and other discussions we had between class in preparing for the next session. The course was taught using Zoom, and I decided not to transcribe these recordings but only watch them to refresh my memory and observe my teaching. I did not transcribe or keep identifiable records of these recordings in order to protect the anonymity of students. Instead, I decided to use a narrative approach to data collection wherein I created field texts on those decisions and discussions that occurred during and between each session of the course (Clandinin & Connelly, 2000).

By field texts, I mean the records of my thinking, observations, action, and dialogue that occurred in each phase. By dialogue, I mean the occasions in which my critical friend and I interrogated and investigated, considered and reconsidered the documents we had collected about teaching. As the course unfolded, I constructed these field texts, taking notes on what was happening in the class, my evaluation of the activities, as well as keeping a record of changes we made, emails or other artifacts that were relevant. Data collected during teaching were an expansion of the materials collected during the first planning phase and represented records of the lived experience of teaching the class. It included notes about the schedule, assignments, major projects, rubrics, and other related artifacts or observations made for the duration of teaching the class. Because the process of coming to know was dialogue, understandings about my teacher educator knowledge and the shifts in them occurred as part of these discussions and were included in my field texts.

Debriefing took place at the end of most sessions and again as we met to prepare for the next one. It also occurred as we reflected on what had happened, evaluated what worked with course design and student interactions, and delegated the upcoming tasks. Sometimes, reflecting was more like venting as I reacted to something that happened in class, and other times, the thinking was more carefully captured using notetaking and dialogue as we talked over assignments, group progress, interactions, and questioned choices made. Each of us kept an open notebook with a pencil or pen as the class proceeded. The notes we took were not extensive but just a word or two, something which would allow us to recount our thinking when class ended. Then, we referred to these notes about glitches, things we should attend to, and wonderings after the students left.

After Teaching. When the course ended, data were the field notes and other resulting field texts that emerged from discussions and dialogue that took place between and post-teaching. At this point, I revisited initial discussions, in a form of cyclic data collecting, in order to create interim research texts. Interim research texts are more formal and refined documents than field texts that often link data collected with interpretation, and Clandinin and Connelly (2000) noted that these often end up as part of the final report of the study.

After the last session, Stefinee Pinnegar and I met specifically to reflect on the course and for me to consider my own teacher educator knowledge in an online context. This combination of immediate debriefing and final debriefing produced different kinds of questions, stories, and discussion. As I engaged in the process, ideas and concepts emerged. As this occurred and either of us had ideas about what we realized we knew as teacher educators, we would confer with each other. We asked each other to provide evidence that supported any assertion the other made of teacher educator knowledge. Finally, I spent some time reflecting on the course and teacher educator knowledge, journaling, and summarizing my understandings in reflection documents.

In this final phase, I met with Stefinee Pinnegar acting as a critical friend and notes from these discussions bound the data. The process of this inquiry and interpretation was based in dialogue as a process of coming to know, allowing more than one interpretation and multiple meanings (Pinnegar & Hamilton, 2015). Therefore, the data collected after teaching involved constructing interim research texts to revisit previous understandings about teacher educator knowledge. These included written notes, journaling, or other forms of communication I used to capture our thinking about teacher educator knowledge. In this final phase, findings emerged as I developed assertions of my understanding about teacher educator knowledge. Therefore, part of this phase included strategies for establishing trustworthiness concerning the assertions about teacher educator knowledge we were making.

Data Analysis

It is clear from the previous explanation of data collection that analysis of the experience I had in planning, teaching, and reflecting on an online course was an ongoing process closely connected to data collection. But to reiterate, analysis followed a format of dialogue as described by Pinnegar and Hamilton (2015). Like a constant comparative method (Glaser & Strauss, 1967/2017), there was an ongoing iteration of data collection and analysis. Also like a constant comparative method, findings and themes were grounded in data. Unlike a constant comparative method, I did not envision the process of data collection and emerging theory as a spiraling data-to-category-to-concept process. Rather, I employed dialogue as defined as a tool for knowing in intimate scholarship (Pinnegar & Hamilton, 2015). As Pinnegar and Hamilton stated, "In intimate scholarship, understanding emerges as we engage with participants, the data we collect, and our own knowledge and understanding" (p. 146). A dialogue

EXPLORING TEACHER EDUCATOR KNOWLEDGE 47

approach is "oriented toward inquiry and reflection and necessarily involves both critique and response with evidence" (p. 147).

By carefully recording data at each of the three phases of planning, teaching, and reflecting, I and my critical friend noticed common themes or interesting connections, even early in data collection. Then in our dialogue, we interrogated these understandings and sought for further corroboration. Unlike other methods, I did not wait to start asking what I knew but discussed what I saw as I went along, interrogated it, and revisited it. Once we noted a theme, as we went forward in our discussion, we constantly sought other evidence to support or unsettle this theme. It made us awake to that theme and its nuances in our data and in our experience. Thus, using dialogue, I kept records of understandings and evidence of the data that supported them and continued to question those findings before teaching, during teaching, and after teaching the course. Seven major strands of teacher educator knowledge were identified, described, and interrogated during the stages of planning, teaching, and reflecting.

To encourage deeper reflection, multiple perspectives, and strengthen trustworthiness, Stefinee Pinnegar, as my critical friend, interrogated my assertions as I interrogated hers. As I developed findings, I continued to act, reflect, and debrief. One voice in the research that was often questioned was my own. As I made assertions, I checked the data collected for meaning and questioned it using my own skeptical internal voice. The voice of Stefinee Pinnegar acting as the critical friend was vital as she corroborated or raised objections. A third voice important for dialogue that was considered as the data collection continued was the voice of findings from research that supported or contradicted the common themes or findings that emerged at each stage.

The next step in my analysis involved composing the analytic narrative vignettes. As I examined my own experience and knowledge as a teacher educator, I analyzed the data and the major understandings of what comprised my teacher educator knowledge. However, those understandings were entangled with each other within my field texts. I decided that in order to untangle the seven strands of teacher educator knowledge, a good strategy would be to construct analytic narrative vignettes that contained within them the constellation of major understandings. Based on the analysis, I composed three narrative vignettes representing each of the three ongoing stages of planning, teaching, and reflecting as well as the constellation of understandings.

In Chapter 4, I will explain the process of developing analytic narrative vignettes. Then, in order to make visible my teacher educator knowledge, findings from the vignettes are analyzed in Chapter 5, so that the reader may see how the major understandings were evident in my experiences and thinking. The strands are teased apart, and definitions of these aspects of my teacher educator knowledge begin to take shape in each context. Following the recommendation of Saldaña (2016), as I analyzed each of the narrative vignettes, I used an italicized font for each of the themes as they are addressed. In this way, "salient and important ideas do not escape the reader's notice.... Also, the tactic is a way of confirming for yourself that your data analysis has reached a stage of synthesis and crystallization" (p. 282).

In the vignettes and in the analysis of them, my critical friend is also the co-teacher of the course. In Chapter 5, she is sometimes referred to as Dr Pinnegar, most often in the teaching vignette when acting in her formal role as professor. Most often though, I refer to her as Stefinee, in order to emphasize the collegial tone of our critical friendship and represent the more informal pattern of our dialogue.

Again, the data were collected and analyzed beginning in planning the curriculum for the TELL 440 class, continuing as I taught the course (co-teaching with Dr Pinnegar) and culminating in reflecting where we critically examined our decisions, debriefing after every class session and at the end of the course. There were several recurring topics that developed in depth and nuance as I engaged in dialogue with my critical friend. In the move from field texts to narrative vignettes, I came to understand the ways my analysis of these topics both enlarged and enlightened my teacher educator knowledge. Like turning points (Bullock & Ritter, 2011), my major understandings relate to a process of recording and developing understandings. Finally, the work of considering how the seven strands of teacher educator knowledge unfolded in each vignette helped me see how the strands wound together throughout and helped me explicate the findings.

Trustworthiness and Rigor

In S-STEP research, when the researcher is also the researched, trustworthiness is established at the very conception of the research project in the framing of the research question and in the literature review itself (Hamilton et al., 2020). As a scholar I am committed to demonstrating my thoroughness and integrity by composing and researching carefully the question, the context, and the methods chosen for investigation. As I have stated, I relied on a critical friend to increase trustworthiness. In this study, Stefinee Pinnegar's role of critical friendship kept the study focused on the research question, kept the researcher (myself) in a skeptical stance, and proposed critique and multiple interpretations in ways that broadened and deepened my initial understandings. Findings that emerge from dialogue with a critical friend can have more verity through discussion, critique, and establishing links to theory and other research. Just as with any research endeavor, trustworthiness was then established by my rigor as researcher, writer, and scholar, and my ability to express my research question and purpose, present the current state of relevant issues and research, and adequately describe my methods for arriving at any interpretations.

Because the study's focus was on one researcher's experience, I knew it was important to make links to the larger research conversation explicit and clear. I attempted to address this concern with a comprehensive literature review. It was important to build a broad knowledge base of teacher education practices and rich understanding of research focused on teacher educator knowledge. This cannot be done if the research remains localized and if I do not adequately explain how this research relates to the larger research context in teacher education. Similarly, it was important to make links to other research strands, looking for commonalities and ways for research in different contexts to inform each other. Another weakness in some qualitative research is to inadequately reveal the methods used to arrive at findings, which I have addressed here by critiquing the rigor of my methods and especially by making transparent my data collection and analysis tools. This is further established through Chapter 4 where I clearly describe the construction of analytic narrative vignettes. Finally, when making claims or assertions about my own teacher educator knowledge, it is important to explicitly connect the data to the interpretations I claim, which I addressed through the use of analytic narrative vignettes and the monitoring influence of a critical friend.

HOW CAN ANALYTIC NARRATIVE VIGNETTES ALLOW COMPLEX REPRESENTATION OF DATA?

ABSTRACT

Analytic narrative vignettes are exemplars of the data in a study. When confronted with large data sets of narrative and expository text, researchers are faced with the challenge of how to present their data and findings in a way that is easily comprehensible. One strategy for making complex and large amounts of narrative data accessible is to create exemplars, known as analytic narrative vignettes. This chapter frames the theoretical foundation of analytical narrative vignettes in a discussion about when using exemplars may be useful. For qualitative researchers with large data sets of accounts or interviews, exemplars have the potential to capture findings in a more accessible narrative representation of the data. In addition, the narrative vignettes serve as another cycle of analysis. Using the context of my study on teacher educator knowledge, I will outline the decision-making and process of composing vignettes and their usefulness beyond simple representation to capture complex findings. It is important to employ narrative elements that will invite the reader to experience the story. Just a few to consider are setting, narrative viewpoint, dialogue, plot, an awareness of audience, and for narrative vignettes, a lean toward simplicity.

Keywords: Analytic narrative vignettes; exemplars; data analysis; narrative research; qualitative research; teacher educator knowledge; pedagogical content knowledge; milieu; personal practical knowledge; tacit knowledge

In this chapter, the purposes and construction of analytic narrative vignettes are explored and explained. In my study on teacher educator knowledge, certain understandings about my own teacher educator knowledge emerged in the process of planning for, teaching, and reflecting on an online course for preservice teachers. Evidence for the strands of teacher educator knowledge was exemplified through analytic narrative vignettes based on the data. The composition raised the status of this evidence to exemplars (Mishler, 1990). In this chapter, I will provide a theoretical basis for the usefulness of creating exemplars in qualitative

---

Exploring Teacher Educator Knowledge
Advances in Research on Teaching, Volume 48, 51–62
Copyright © 2025 Celina Dulude Lay
Published under exclusive licence by Emerald Publishing Limited
ISSN: 1479-3687/doi:10.1108/S1479-368720240000048004

data analysis, particularly when large data sets need to be presented and utilized as evidence. Then I will explain the process of representing data in an analytic narrative vignette. In explaining the construction process I utilized in developing narrative vignettes, I will provide some of the raw data from this study and make evident the decision process I engaged in as I composed a vignette as well as my learning from participation in this next stage of analysis.

BENEFITS OF EXEMPLARS

The use of an exemplar, in this case an analytic narrative vignette, is a technique to summarize and capture the analysis and emerging themes of a large and robust data set into a brief narrative representation. Mishler (1990) stated that exemplars can be useful for interpreting and representing data. While exemplars cannot be standardized or removed from their contexts, they can be useful when "...a context-based explication is required of how observations are transformed into data and findings, and of how interpretations are grounded" (p. 423). Because of the length and complexity of the data sets, exemplars were a useful way of presenting clear evidence of the findings that had emerged in this study.

There are some obvious and less obvious benefits to the use of exemplars. Of course, one huge advantage of an exemplar is that it makes a molehill out of a mountain (of field notes). In quantitative representations of data, the same issue can occur in which the findings are clear to the researcher, but unless the data analysis results are conveyed visually in a pleasing and simple-to-grasp representation, the research may remain uncompelling to a reader and its significance overlooked, unclear, or not understood. Boy et al. (2014) emphasized the value of and the ability to turn a research question specified and explored in the data domain into a graphic or pictorial image. The benefits of visually appealing data representation of statistical data, for example, through the use of charts, plots, and graphs are obvious, particularly in a world that grapples with vast amounts of data generated daily.

In quantitative work, it is that clever but clear representation of numbers in charts and graphs that make clear the persuasive evidence for the findings presented and in qualitative work; the words to represent findings may be so large that it is difficult to present the clear picture that is needed. Therefore, a challenge in qualitative research is the burden of many words. One strategy qualitative researchers may use is the reporting of findings using numerical or graphic representations of the coding. The risk in taking this approach is the reduction of richness of detail and context as well as nuance of information gleaned in the data. Yet readers are not willing or able to sift through all the relevant text in order to be persuaded. Thus, a narrative representation of vast amounts of text can make a researcher's exploration and analysis more accessible to readers. Moving from the large body of data to a well-crafted narrative representation enables the researcher to verify the presence of the analysis they had made and raise the data representation to exemplar status, as well as clarify the connection between the evidence and the findings.

EXPLORING TEACHER EDUCATOR KNOWLEDGE

Another advantage of using exemplars is that they give a researcher an added ability to honor the research context. Erickson (1986) explained that by making an exemplar or report that represents the evidence, "the sights and sounds of what was being said and done are described in the natural sequence of their occurrence in real time. The moment-to-moment style of description in a narrative vignette gives the reader a sense of being there in the scene" (p. 150). Erickson further described a narrative vignette as a "vivid portrayal" of the collected and represented data.

Much of the value of a qualitative study is in the study of the data in a particular context, with particular local features. Clandinin and Connelly (2000), when presenting narrative inquiry as a method and methodology, emphasized the importance of always being aware of the three-dimensional narrative space. The three dimensions of the narrative space include: interaction, with one's self and others; continuity, moving through time in the past, present, and future; and situation, an awareness of place or setting. By using an exemplar to represent the collected data within the three-dimensional narrative space, the researcher is effectively highlighting the value of the participants involved, as well as recognizing the particular place and time that the research was conducted.

Another perhaps less obvious benefit of exemplars is that they provide another cycle of analysis. When I chose to write analytic narrative vignettes to represent my data, my collected data included 10 recorded Zoom classes, transcripts of at least 20 hour-long meetings with my co-teacher and critical friend, journaled records of my own thinking and study, more than 100 direct messages and email, and constructed artifacts such as course assignments, assessments, and required readings. As I attempted to grapple with how to make clear what I had found based on accurate representation of the evidence of those findings, my focus was directed to solving the problem of how to talk about the data, how to show how the themes were indeed grounded in the data, and represent field notes, stories, and discussion in a manageable way.

However, as I set about creating my exemplars, I found that this process was not just about representation. Since I had to determine how to write a narrative that vividly portrayed the evidence, I went back over the data, remembering the interactions and decisions that had occurred. In this way, the act of writing served to deepen my thinking about the strands of teacher educator knowledge I had encountered. Just as a data visualization graphic for a quantitative study can provide a support for further analysis by highlighting patterns or outliers, an analytic narrative vignette can act as more than just a convenient representation of the data. In the making of exemplars, identified patterns and themes or new perspectives can potentially provide further understanding of the findings.

Following a vignette, the next step in reporting is to unpack, explain, and assert findings. Analytic narrative vignettes are a useful way to represent evidence for readers and provide a format for unpacking and explaining. Unlike a common format for reporting findings by listing themes with pertinent quotes to provide support, this method means the themes are embedded in a contextualized and holistic format.

Rather than giving a sense of coding, by expounding the themes through analytic narrative vignettes, the researcher maintains a sense of narrative, while anchoring the reported findings in a situated context. Saldaña (2016) recommends that for writing the analysis to use a bolded font for each of the themes as they are addressed. I followed this recommendation and found that the process of composing analytic narrative vignettes and then using a vignette to unpack and assert findings provided not just the "vivid portrayal" that Erickson (1986) described, but also that salient information did not escape notice. The process of unpacking the vignette and highlighting the themes helps readers follow your thinking but also, according to Saldaña (2016), "...is a way of confirming for yourself that your data analysis has reached a stage of synthesis and crystallization" (p. 282).

Thus, another benefit of exemplars is that they are a further check to trustworthiness. I had transcriptions, field notes, and mountains of raw data, but the act of deciding which events to collapse, retell, or include required careful consideration and the decision to involve a critical friend to read my vignettes for accuracy and honest representation. Then, the process of using the vignettes to explain and illustrate the strands of teacher educator knowledge allowed me the chance to carefully consider the salient features of the experience of uncovering teacher educator knowledge and confirmation that the themes were indeed present and resonant in the data and in my thinking.

THE PROCESS OF CAPTURING THEMES

I took a history class as an undergraduate that required us to report our thoughts about required class readings in the form of "capture" papers. Sometime into my experience writing analytic narrative vignettes for this study, I remembered and reflected back on the experience of writing those capture papers. For example, in the course, we were assigned excerpts from Herodotus, Navajo creation stories, and the Bible, and I would attempt to capture the grand 19-year-old insights about human history that had emerged in my thoughts while I read.

Similar to that analytical attempt to capture the understandings and connections of a text, my use of analytic narrative vignettes for this research represents descriptive moments in time, in order to capture the experience and thinking of a research process. The intent is not to compose a short story with a well-articulated plot and characters, but rather to provide a narrative glimpse. In other words, you have collected your data, you have done much analysis, you know your major strands or themes, and now you aim to "capture" all of that economically in a descriptive narrative.

It is important to note that data analysis does not occur after writing the vignettes. It has occurred already and continues during the composition and consideration of vignettes. Also, the account itself is an analysis.

In organizing and considering the field notes from my study, I focused on moments in planning, teaching, and reflecting that were captured in our notes. This organization emerged as a natural chronological way to organize the data. These three stages of planning, teaching, and reflecting then became a useful way to focus the three-dimensional narrative space (time, setting, people) – which also, significantly, revealed that the strands of teacher educator knowledge identified were relevant and in play during each and all the stages of preparing for and

EXPLORING TEACHER EDUCATOR KNOWLEDGE

teaching the course. Each of the three vignettes is intended to capture the major understandings about teacher educator knowledge but not necessarily include every example from the field texts, simply those that provided the strongest evidence. I represent these major understandings as seven strands of teacher educator knowledge, represented in each narrative vignette. The seven strands are: *Content Knowledge, Fixed and Fluid Elements, Knowledge of Milieu, Pedagogical Intent, Preservice Teacher Knowledge and Belief, Value and Fragility of Relationships,* and *Theory Matters.* For reference, the definitions and theoretical underpinnings of the seven strands are listed below.

Descriptions of Strands of Teacher Educator Knowledge

Content Knowledge	Associated with Shulman's work on pedagogical content knowledge, the expertise a teacher educator holds on subject matter as well as the professional understanding of how to engage learners with the subject matter. Also emerging from Schwab's conception of the commonplaces of an educational setting, that teachers and learners interact with the content in a given milieu (Craig, 2008; Schwab, 1973).
Fixed and Fluid Elements	There are elements of a course design that can be set and fixed and others that can vary. Decisions about what to fix and what to allow to vary reveal the theoretical underpinnings of a course designer and purposes of a course.
Knowledge of Milieu	Also related to Schwab's work, in curriculum design, the milieu is important to consider along with the teacher, the student, and the subject matter. Indeed, attending to the settings and environments of learners and teachers becomes just as integral to curriculum-making as subject matter expertise.
Pedagogical Intent	A term taken from Allman and Pinnegar's (2020) research. Identifying pedagogical intent is an endeavor of a teacher educator to align competing goals of delivery of content and teaching practice. Teacher educators target an intended *learning experience* hoped to be accomplished when assigning a learning task, thus informing the selection of content, activities, and, if designing online, digital tools.
Preservice Teacher Knowledge and Belief	Associated with Clandinin's (2000) assertions about teachers' personal practical knowledge, this knowledge comes from a recognition that preservice teachers know a lot about teaching, and a teacher educator's role is to help shape and reshape the knowledge they already have. Teacher educators identify those teacher education practices particularly attuned to supporting changes and growth in preservice teacher knowledge and belief.
Value and Fragility of Relationships	In a socio-relational course design now shifted to an online format, knowledge a teacher educator may hold for developing teacher–student relationships, and especially for supporting student learning communities.
Theory Matters	A recognition that theory underlies and drives a teacher educator's decisions related to pedagogy, content, technology, and relationships. In unpacking, understandings about the nature of knowledge and how learning occurs in educational environments emerge.

56 *How Narrative Vignettes Allow Representation of Data?*

Now that the context of the study is clearer and the purpose of vignettes outlined, in this next step, I will provide some raw data and demonstrate how it may be analyzed, interpreted, and composed as a vignette.

The following field notes are from a planning meeting on April 11, 2020 along with another from a meeting on April 22, 2020. Stefinee and I met to make decisions on course materials and assignments and to set up the course online. We invited our teaching assistant (TA) to participate in this planning meeting as well. I took notes of our discussion throughout and then summarized our conversation points in an outline. The outline is constructed as a chronicle of the event (Clandinin & Connelly, 2000). For the purposes of this chapter, I have added detail to the document, attending to coherence to make the meanings clearer. For example, I changed our TA's name, added punctuation and better spelling, and completed some incomplete sentences and added detail where needed for clarity.

Excerpt of Field Notes From the Planning Phase

April 11, 2020 (Stefinee Pinnegar, Celina Lay, and Karrie our TA)

(1) Constructing the new Teaching English Language Learners (TELL) course –
Stefinee: they [preservice teachers] are different from [in-service] public school teachers
- The sense I have that things have to build on each other and you don't reteach – you expect students to learn it the first time and you provide refreshers, support, resources, and reminders that they know this
- Frozen/fixed course elements: you have to make sure you have identified and put in place the key ideas you want covered, and unlike in face to face, you can't adjust it at the course level (producer level) at the last minute
- You have to think of everything they need.
(2) Celina – front time in planning. Their obligation as adult learners and my obligation to them. We expect them to be prepared for class. Not comfortable with Zoom and they have to come having done their work. My obligation is not – wait a minute while I find this. Have I thought of everything we will need? They have to be prepared or we cannot move content forward. There's not space to draw forward what they didn't do from their fellow students
(3) Planning – moving a course we have taught face to face to online – we have assignments we love, and we have to rethink how vital they are for students even having a meaningful class interaction – Is this the best way to teach the ideas we want them to learn, and is this the best activity for online? Because we have both taught this before, then we sort of know what they don't learn. We have figured out what is basic and what they have difficulty learning.
(4) One "aha" is working with Karrie who had TA's twice [for TELL classes] and taken this class once. I find myself thinking Oh I need to ask Karrie about . . . Corpus study (What did you learn?) It's also why we added having them share a favorite part of the Standards for Effective Pedagogy (SEP) –

EXPLORING TEACHER EDUCATOR KNOWLEDGE

(5) Getting-to-know-students routine (there's not enough time), assessment (about our instituting the SEP reflection at the beginning).

(6) We wonder should we have them post on digital board one idea from the Sheltered Instruction Observation Protocol (SIOP) chapters. Right as they enter. One idea. We should label the post (We will be open 10 minutes before)

(7) As I'm trying to transition this over, I'm trying to draw on other formats – project-based learning. Multiple, Simultaneous, Diverse, Learning Activity (MSDLA) – thinking I don't know Stefinee: You have to have a rubric. You have to think about all the parts and whether you have provided all the knowledge or ways to draw forward what they know. You have to find ways to make them comfortable with all the uncertainty. We are wondering how we will do this online. We have lots of experience with this – so this is one of the things with project-based learning

(8) Project-based learning – for our program the formal learning started with Sec Ed 276. (Stefinee: My learning goes back to the Architecture classroom when I was Sarah's TA and interviewed Kirby.) Celina: Joyce Nelson was really important to my learning.

I recognized that part of this process is attending carefully to evidence that would support assertions about the strands of teacher educator knowledge. Thus, constructing the vignette is also a process that extends analysis and supports the trustworthiness of the interpretation of the data. As self-study researchers, we sometimes overlook the fact that part of demonstrating trustworthiness is not just for external audiences but also for establishing the credibility of the interpretation to myself, the researcher. Notice how evidence for the strands was evident in this segment in data.

Support for the strand of *Content Knowledge* is evident when we are deciding how to have students learn the content of the SIOP model (Echevarria et al., 2012).

Knowledge of Milieu is evident as we articulate the purpose of the meeting – to plan to teach a course online. It is also present in our discussion of how best to prepare preservice teachers during a worldwide pandemic in learning the content of integrating content with literacy and language learning in K-12.

Thoughts of *Theory* that form my theoretical underpinnings are hinted at when we discuss the way we think learning happens, "the sense I have that things have to build on each other" (Item 1.a). We also discuss methods of teaching, beliefs, and our memories of formative teachers and experiences with project-based learning.

Pedagogical Intent is in play during instances of making decisions about assignments, specifically when we wrestle with how a particular learning goal can best be reached with the assignment as we shift it online (Item 3). We also begin to question whether certain assignments are worth the effort as designed, or if they would even engage students effectively in reaching the intended learning goal.

Fixed and Fluid Elements are mentioned explicitly and almost immediately in our meeting, referred to as frozen/fixed content elements (Item 1.b), as we are reminded or perhaps confronted with the realization that we will not have the same ability to adjust in the moment if an assignment is going awry.

Preservice Teacher Knowledge and Belief as a theme is evident here in an unusual way. I was accustomed to being aware of my students' teacher knowledge they bring to the classroom, but in this planning stage, I do not yet know the specific students for this class but I do have knowledge of preservice teachers based on all of courses Stefinee and I have taught. More importantly, I have a teaching assistant who also happens to be very familiar with the content and assignments in the course and is articulate in representing her own knowledge. In my "aha" (Item 4), it is evident that Karrie's knowledge of the course from a student perspective will be helpful as we make decisions in what to include, omit, and change.

Finally, the theme of the *Value and Fragility of Relationships* is hinted at as we grapple with the realization that there is not enough time for getting to know students (Item 5). We also discuss (Item 7) the understanding we have that students who feel comfortable in class are more willing to engage in challenging activities.

Implicit or explicit discussions of each of the seven strands of teacher educator knowledge are indicated in this extracted piece of data from the planning phase. Looking back at this outline summary of our meeting, it is exciting to see the evidence so clear and so powerful. However, when this meeting was held and this summary outline written, I had not yet reached a place of settled findings. Nor was I even thinking of the data collection process in terms of three stages of planning, teaching, and reflecting. At the time of constructing the chronicle, the strands and ways to articulate them were still in an emerging phase. It is through engaging in this process of reviewing the data to represent it that strands and the evidence supporting them became clarified.

We held another meeting 10 days later to finish preparing the class and building the course on the learning management platform. This field note represents my own reflections and notes made after the meeting, and I turned it into a research text modeled on the form of a chronicle (Clandinin & Connelly, 2000). Therefore, I cleaned up my typos and added bracketed clarification in a few places, but at this point, it was not necessary to understand the complete context and all of the details. In other words, my note may make more sense to me than it does to the reader. I will present the data excerpt and show how the strands of teacher educator knowledge continue to weave their way through the data.

April 22, 2020 (Meeting with Stefinee Pinnegar and Celina Lay)

Helpful to make a more direct link between the MSDLA [Multiple, Simultaneous, Diverse, Learning Activity] and what we are teaching each session. We have always attended to everything they need to put in the final TELL project but we did not make it explicit enough for students. Or methodical enough. We weren't systematic about making those connections clear. I think when students were taking all the TELL courses, they were used

EXPLORING TEACHER EDUCATOR KNOWLEDGE

to the format but since we only get them in TELL 440 using the TELL curriculum, we realized it has to be more explicit. There needs to be a connection between what I'm teaching them and how they are going to take it up in their final project and therefore in their regular teaching. What becomes clear with CBL [Content Based Instruction] is that constructing this curriculum has lots of moving pieces. Hidden curriculum and enacted curriculum, all these pieces need to be more systematically incorporated. Schwab, student-teacher – context-cultural milieu. What Stef learned from Walter Doyle is that every bit of that comes back around to the task, embedded in the task you have given students to work on. Task moves to task is Dewey. It's also the Rodgers work on presence. Because we educated in groups, when we attend to a child, they need our undivided attention. So our tasks need to be able to run by themselves so that we can attend. That's why we've always had facilitators. I've realized working with one colleague that she has let go of those cumulative pieces that were in the original family class and lost sight of the potential level of learning of students coming to the class.

In this note, it is clear that I am still considering how best to construct an online curriculum that reveals the learning goals and makes content connections more explicit (*Content Knowledge, Pedagogical Intent*). Unlike in the first meeting where the strand of *Theory* is only inferred, it is interesting to note that in this discussion, *Theory Matters* are at the forefront of our thinking, including a theoretical evaluation of the TELL program we have been so involved in and detailed references to ideas and educational researchers who have influenced us, such as Schwab (1973), Doyle (1990), Dewey (2007), and (Rodgers & Raider-Roth, 2006). At this stage, the strands of teacher educator knowledge are still emerging and being articulated and refined for me.

By the time I taught the course and was reflecting on how it went and what I learned, these ideas had come up repeatedly and resonated with me. In fact, I felt confident that they captured my own teacher educator knowledge. During analysis and creation of exemplars, it is important to note that not only are emerging themes becoming more solid, but other strands may also become evident. Then, I determined to write the three vignettes to represent three stages of Planning, Teaching, and Reflecting. This was done by looking back over the data for planning, teaching, or reflecting and considering a way to reveal the strands within a narrative representation of the three-dimensional narrative space I had lived. Although I do not think I thought about it in quite those terms, the constructing of a narrative vignette became clear as I engaged in that process.

COMPOSING A VIGNETTE

The Planning Vignette is presented and analyzed in Chapter 5, so I will not repeat all of it here. However, beginning with a brief excerpt of the Planning Vignette, I will demonstrate how the data fed into the narrative constructed. It will be clear how the narrative creates a representation of the three-dimensional narrative space, in this instance, the setting of a meeting of colleagues in the time before the course was taught in the spring of 2020. I begin by presenting the first few paragraphs of the narrative vignette for planning.

Excerpt From the Planning Vignette

The two of us met together at Stefinee's kitchen table to plan our online class, with our teaching assistant joining in via Zoom. Immediately, the three of us began attending to the pressing questions. I looked down at one of my open screens, "I'm keeping a list. What is everything we need ready by the first day?" Karrie and Stefinee also started their own lists of reminders and assignments to add to the learning platform and schedule. As we kicked around ideas, walking through each session, we continued to assess and re-evaluate each of the activities in the course and the learning trajectory. Our continual focus was on what was essential and what was merely important.

I groaned while trying to shuffle through ten open windows on my laptop. "All the parts! Have you noticed that with every assignment we keep coming back to what we want them to learn, how to enact it online, and what kind of support they'll need?"

Stefinee agreed. "Because we have taught this before, we sort of know what they learn, and what they don't learn. In other words, I have already figured out which concepts are basic and which they have difficulty learning. Karrie, you just took this class last year. What do you think? How are we doing?"

Karrie explained that now as a TA she understands all the moving parts, but as a student the point of each activity was not always clear. When she said this, I thought, "How can I do better? How can I make the purpose of each activity clear?"

When composing narrative vignettes, a key reminder is to remember that you were there but your audience wasn't. Just like when writing personal essay, it's helpful to employ narrative elements that will invite the reader in. Just a few to consider are setting, narrative viewpoint, dialogue, plot, awareness of audience, and for narrative vignettes, a lean toward simplicity.

Add a Little Setting. Just Enough

The vignette begins, "The two of us met together at Stefinee's kitchen table to plan our online class, with our teaching assistant joining in via Zoom." This was a typical place for our meetings, and you can easily picture an informal setting between two colleagues and one TA joining on Zoom, laptops on the table, ready to plan. Later, "I groaned while trying to shuffle through 10 open windows on my laptop." Just one sentence captures the visual image (and sound) of me in front of my laptop and some of the frustration and complexity of the task.

Choose a Point of View

Since this research was a self-study of my own practice, it was appropriate to narrate the vignettes from a first-person point of view. For example, in the vignette, my point of view is evident in this response to the TA, "When she said this, I thought, 'How can I do better? How can I make the purpose of each activity clear?'" I am positioning myself as researcher who also has a role as a character in the story. A first-person viewpoint can be more intimate and personal, which in this case matches the intimate scholarship stance.

EXPLORING TEACHER EDUCATOR KNOWLEDGE 61

Consider How to Use Dialogue
I begin with, "I'm keeping a list." I have no idea if those were my exact words, but I probably said something similar. Beginning this way makes the vignette the story of a real meeting and fills out my character a little, placing me as the organizer of tasks within the group. In another example, dialogue allows the themes to be revealed. Stefinee asks, "Karrie, you just took this class last year. What do you think? How are we doing?" Our field notes show that I had realized on April 11, early on, that Karrie's contributions would be invaluable. When *Preservice Teacher Knowledge and Belief* emerged as a strong strand of teacher educator knowledge, I wanted to highlight this unique way we had enacted this strand from the beginning, during Planning. The crafted dialogue with Stefinee inviting Karrie's ideas emphasizes this, as does my inner dialogue wondering how I can "do better," specifically, how I can modify assignments based on Karrie's feedback.

Craft a Simple Plot
Since the provided vignette excerpt is incomplete, the sequence of events does not completely unfold, but one can see how the meeting begins and can anticipate that perhaps the vignette may end with the end of the meeting. (Chapter 5 Spoiler Alert. It does). Because the vignette follows a simple plot of beginning, middle, and end of a meeting, it's easy to learn about who the characters of the story are without too much detail to complicate the story. Instead, I include just a little about our worries, beliefs, and ideas as we work on designing the online course. For a vignette, a simple plot allows readers a path to follow, to walk with the characters through the tensions, challenges, solutions, and resolutions that will reveal themes.

Awareness of Audience
There is a tension in trying to scrupulously represent the participants and the context of a research project while condensing all of this into a narrative representation that a newcomer can follow. An awareness of audience, an ability to see our writing through another's eyes, is important to any researcher/writer, but when using narrative exemplars, it is especially important to represent the data in a way that will clearly convey findings. In order to illustrate this point, let me state that I teach at a private religious university, and most of the faculty and students share a common religion. Because of this, we also have shared cultural norms that may be more obscuring or distracting to my purpose of illuminating strands of teacher educator knowledge if I were to include such details in a narrative vignette. For the most part, I omitted these religious references when composing my vignettes, making the decision that details that need explaining are too burdensome.

If, on the other hand, an analytic narrative vignette *needs* to include unique or unfamiliar aspects in order to accurately represent findings, then audience awareness helps researchers choose the particular details that will reveal to readers the three-dimensional narrative space, support readers in understanding an unknown setting, and reduce confusion. For example, this study took place during the worldwide COVID-19 pandemic. While not specifically mentioned in this excerpt, the complete vignette contains details that capture the unusual circumstances of this time, such as the fact that the teaching and planning takes place not at an institution or office setting but at a kitchen table. Also, the mention of my laptop having many tabs open hints at the difficulties of moving an in-person class to an online platform.

Keep the Story Simple to Highlight the Data

There is no need to represent in the narrative all the ways the data were collected and analyzed. I kept the narrative focused into one event, a meeting at a kitchen table, and set about including threads that would weave together a coherent picture of the thematic strands. I used exposition judiciously, sometimes summing up information or the result of a discussion in a few sentences. For example, "As we kicked around ideas, walking through each session, we continued to assess and re-evaluate each of the activities in the course and the learning trajectory. Our continual focus was on what was essential and what was merely important." The words "essential and what was merely important" are an echo of conversations we had throughout Planning and into the Teaching and Reflecting stages too. Summing up this idea in exposition accurately represents multiple conversations and the navigation of the process we went through to determine course assignments and how to spend class time.

In conclusion, there are critical decisions to be made in the research and analysis process when analytical narrative vignettes are going to be employed. It is helpful to understand what an analytical narrative vignette is and what it is not. Then, researchers can determine if the use of such exemplars would potentially be beneficial in their research context and with their data. Again, the process of representing data with an exemplar is itself a continuation of interpretation of that data. In addition, a researcher's awareness of audience as they employ narrative elements to compose a vignette aids in that continued interpretation and adds a layer of confirmation and trustworthiness to the research endeavor. Thus, a compelling purpose of a vignette is to provide a clearer, simpler way to represent comprehensive data sets, but these other benefits should not be overlooked.

WHAT DOES THE PLANNING VIGNETTE REVEAL ABOUT TEACHER EDUCATOR KNOWLEDGE?

ABSTRACT

The strands of teacher educator knowledge are explained using an analytic narrative vignette to represent data collected during the planning of an online course in the spring of 2020. The Planning Vignette represents a meeting of two colleagues planning a course together while an undergraduate teaching assistant joins the meeting on Zoom. The Planning Vignette is analyzed systematically by highlighting the themes as they appeared and noting, when evident, how they interrelated with each other. In this way, I am able to show how the strands of teacher educator knowledge were evident from the beginning, in the process of course design. Following analysis is a summary of insights that emerged from examining my teacher educator knowledge during the planning stage. Each of the seven strands of teacher educator knowledge is discussed.

Keywords: Teacher educator knowledge; curriculum design; online teacher education; teacher education; pedagogical intent; pedagogical content knowledge; milieu; preservice teacher knowledge; TESOL K-12; project-based course design

In this chapter, the major understandings about teacher educator knowledge are presented, with a particular focus on the Planning Vignette. I represent these major understandings as strands of teacher educator knowledge that emerged in the process of planning, teaching, and reflecting on the course. These strands of teacher educator knowledge were developed as I constructed analytic narrative vignettes based on the data. As I constructed these vignettes, I focused on moments in planning, teaching, and reflecting that were captured in our notes. The process of composing expands these vignettes to exemplar status (Mishler, 1990). While planning the course, the data revealed my understanding of the strands, represented in the vignette. Next, in Chapter 6, the vignette on Teaching

---

Exploring Teacher Educator Knowledge
Advances in Research on Teaching, Volume 48, 63–75
Copyright © 2025 Celina Dulude Lay
Published under exclusive licence by Emerald Publishing Limited
ISSN: 1479-3687/doi:10.1108/S1479-368720240000048005

highlights how these strands of teacher educator knowledge were revealed and how they entwined and informed each other while teaching the course online. Then, in Chapter 7, the Reflecting Vignette captures how these strands of teacher educator knowledge were represented in my action and thinking beyond the teaching and planning.

Each vignette is intended to capture all of the strands of teacher educator knowledge but not necessarily include every example from the field texts. All seven strands of teacher educator knowledge are represented in each narrative vignette. The seven strands are: *Content Knowledge, Fixed and Fluid Elements, Knowledge of Milieu, Pedagogical Intent, Preservice Teacher Knowledge and Belief, Value and Fragility of Relationships,* and *Theory Matters.* A brief description of each strand is listed below:

Descriptions of Strands of Teacher Educator Knowledge

Content Knowledge	Associated with Shulman's work on pedagogical content knowledge, the expertise a teacher educator holds on subject matter as well as the professional understanding of how to engage learners with the subject matter. Also emerging from Schwab's conception of the commonplaces of an educational setting, that teachers and learners interact with the content in a given milieu (Craig, 2008; Schwab, 1973).
Fixed and Fluid Elements	There are elements of a course design that can be set and fixed and others that can vary. Decisions about what to fix and what to allow to vary reveal the theoretical underpinnings of a course designer and purposes of a course.
Knowledge of Milieu	Also related to Schwab's work, in curriculum design, the milieu is important to consider along with the teacher, the student, and the subject matter. Indeed, attending to the settings and environments of learners and teachers becomes just as integral to curriculum-making as subject matter expertise.
Pedagogical Intent	A term taken from Allman and Pinnegar's (2020) research. Identifying pedagogical intent is an endeavor of a teacher educator to align competing goals of delivery of content and teaching practice. Teacher educators target an intended *learning experience* hoped to be accomplished when assigning a learning task, thus informing the selection of content, activities, and, if designing online, digital tools.
Preservice Teacher Knowledge and Belief	Associated with Clandinin's (2000) assertions about teachers' personal practical knowledge, this knowledge comes from a recognition that preservice teachers know a lot about teaching, and a teacher educator's role is to help shape and reshape the knowledge they already have. Teacher educators identify those teacher education practices particularly attuned to supporting changes and growth in preservice teacher knowledge and belief.
Value and Fragility of Relationships	In a socio-relational course design now shifted to an online format, knowledge a teacher educator may hold for developing teacher–student relationships, and especially for supporting student learning communities.
Theory Matters	A recognition that theory underlies and drives a teacher educator's decisions related to pedagogy, content, technology, and relationships. In unpacking, understandings about the nature of knowledge and how learning occurs in educational environments emerge.

EXPLORING TEACHER EDUCATOR KNOWLEDGE

The strands of teacher educator knowledge were evident from the beginning. As my co-instructor and I met to plan the schedule and redesign the course assignments for an online platform, the data began to reveal areas of teacher educator knowledge that mattered to me.

PLANNING

I begin with an analytic narrative vignette that captured the kind of planning experiences we engaged in and revealed the strands of teacher educator knowledge that emerged in analysis of the data. Then, I provide an analysis of the vignette to make visible and clear to the reader how it provided clear evidence of the strands and of my teacher educator knowledge in action. I conclude the analysis of the Planning Vignette with a summary of how each of the strands of teacher educator knowledge was revealed in both explicit and implicit ways and how they influenced each other.

The Planning Vignette: Planning for Spring With the Online Factor

The two of us met together at Stefinee's kitchen table to plan our online class, with our teaching assistant joining in via Zoom. Immediately, the three of us began attending to the pressing questions. I looked down at one of my open screens, "I'm keeping a list. What is everything we need ready by the first day?" Karrie and Stefinee also started their own lists of reminders and assignments to add to the learning platform and schedule. As we kicked around ideas, walking through each session, we continued to assess and re-evaluate each of the activities in the course and the learning trajectory. Our continual focus was on what was essential and what was merely important.

I groaned while trying to shuffle through 10 open windows on my laptop. "All the parts! Have you noticed that with every assignment we keep coming back to what we want them to learn, how to enact it online, and what kind of support they'll need?"

Stefinee agreed. "Because we have taught this before, we sort of know what they learn, and what they don't learn. In other words, I have already figured out which concepts are basic and which they have difficulty learning. Karrie, you just took this class last year. What do you think? How are we doing?"

Karrie explained that now as a TA, she understands all the moving parts, but as a student, the point of each activity was not always clear. When she said this, I thought, "How can I do better? How can I make the purpose of each activity clear?"

From here we made even more progress. The schedule began to look tidier. A pattern emerged for how each class session would be conducted. Stefinee drew arrows and notes, making her fountain pen fly and filling a notebook with the backward design required to connect every activity and reading to the final project. We assigned Karrie to link a list of resources from past courses for students to access. At one point, we thought we had decided on all the pieces that could be prepared in advance.

Stefinee said, "Based on my conversations and work with Bohdana [a colleague], I'm really concerned about how we are going to be responsive and sociocultural online." Stefinee and I had worked with Bohdana (Allman & Pinnegar, 2020) to construct a completely online version of one of the courses in the endorsement program just a few months earlier. As a result, we already knew how much work it took to build an online course. Stefinee shook her head, "We are used to letting learning emerge as students interact and then our teaching has to be responsive in the moment."

I knew this would be one of our main concerns as we transitioned to online. I said, "We really need to think about what preservice teachers know as they enter this class. We know we won't get it totally right."

Karrie chimed in, "What do you mean we won't get it totally right? We really are almost ready for class."

"True, but every student is different," I said. "You can only learn what you're ready to learn. Some of these students will have a lot of experience working with second language learners and some have none." Karrie's eyebrows rose in interest. "For example, we all vary in our misconceptions about English learners. Some students believe all ESL kids speak very limited English. Others assume all ESL kids are poor."

Karrie nodded, "Oh yeah, I have some of those ideas."

"We all do," Stefinee said. "We can only prepare so much. How we decide what kind of support preservice teachers may need is linked to how we honor our commitment to sociocultural theory. It's hard in this online environment to be flexible in the moment in response to gaps or advances in student knowledge."

The meeting continued. As we discussed each assignment of this project-based course, we questioned the purpose of each and considered what we needed to prepare. I was hesitant about one of our usual assignments, reading chapters from Funds of Knowledge and sharing chapter summaries in a jigsaw activity. "You know," I said, "I love these readings, but the jigsaw assignment always gets rushed. I'm not sure students are ever really able to directly connect this activity to the purposes of the class or the final project."

Stefinee agreed, "It's true. We have always attended to everything they need to put in the final project, but we do not always make it explicit or methodical enough for students to make the connection. Let's think and come back to this."

After acknowledging how much I liked the readings, I reflected on the purposes of our course. We worked on our tasks silently for a few minutes. Stefinee said, "This is about preservice teachers having time to develop their knowledge of working with English learners. I think deciding to increase the project-based focus and making the decision that the group size rather than being five students per group would be three. This means the preservice teachers will have more opportunity to contribute their thinking and all of them will need to take an active role."

EXPLORING TEACHER EDUCATOR KNOWLEDGE

I agreed but then turned the focus back to our discussion of how we would decide what was essential. I said, "Each activity needs to support preservice teachers in developing the knowledge that will allow them to meet our overarching purposes, right? I think that a tool that could help us with this process is using Bohdana's conception of pedagogical intent" (Allman & Pinnegar, 2020).

"Yes," Stefinee said. "As we consider each activity, we can ask ourselves what is the fundamental pedagogical intent of this activity, and is it vital in developing preservice teacher knowledge." After that, it was easier to let go of a favorite assignment. We decided to ditch the jigsaw assignment to allow students more time to engage with each other on activities and homework that week.

Later in the meeting, we had more concerns and stopped frequently, stuck on technology questions. We bounced around a few possibilities.

"Should we have them post one idea on the online discussion board from the SIOP [Sheltered Instruction Observation Protocol: content for teachers of English learners] chapters?"

"That might work."

"We could label the post, open it 10 minutes before class begins."

"OK, but if we do this, why? What does it accomplish? We don't want students to have too many tasks. Besides, we've already made-up questions to guide their reading that do a better job of supporting them in learning about SIOP and won't create a frantic frenzy at the beginning of class."

"OK," I said. "What else are we having them do that class session?"

Again, we ended up not requiring discussion board posts from students, in order to keep the focus on the project goals. Really, our students have plenty to do.

Finally, I leaned back and reached for my Diet Coke. "This is hard work! I am sorry the students had to go home for spring term. But honestly, we were already poised to move this course into an online format so hey, it feels like a bonus that we can spend this time on the details, really questioning the course purposes and design."

"It's true," Stefinee nodded in agreement. "We have a real opportunity here to examine each assignment." She smiled at Karrie. "Also, we have Karrie. She's our secret weapon!"

We turned to Karrie because for us, she represented the preservice teachers we would be teaching. She had just finished taking the course and was in the midst of preparing for her final field experience. Because of Karrie's feedback, we incorporated a new idea that we called a work in progress, or a WIP. The WIP was a template outlining all the pieces of the final project for groups to add to each session and turn into a final curriculum project at the end. The WIP was our TA's suggestion and when she saw it, she was thrilled. "I love it, whatever it's called."

Stefinee and I responded in unison, "WIP."

"That's right. This WIP thing will be super helpful."

"I love it too," I agreed. "A place for groups to gather all the pieces of their curriculum making."

Stefinee continued, "Well, we know how important the rubric is to the final project, outlining all the parts. This is just another way for students to document as they go along and for us to be able to check whether we have provided all the tools for them to draw forward what they know. What I hope is that it will make students comfortable with the uncertainty inherent in project-based learning."

"I think so too," I said. "We expect our students to take creative risks, confronting how they might teach ELs and design lessons for them. It's interesting to think of the connection between their obligations and my own as the teacher. I think one of our obligations is to try to reduce anxiety for them by showing them all the pieces of the final assignment all in one place, right at the start." But enough musing. This meeting was very productive, and both Karrie and Stefinee had another meeting to attend.

"OK women, we have our lists. We'll meet again tomorrow."

"Thanks for going to that Zoom training meeting, Stef. See you."

Analysis of the Planning Vignette

I analyzed the Planning Vignette systematically by highlighting the themes as they appeared and noted, when evident, how they interrelated with each other. In order to draw attention to the meaning of the strands of teacher educator knowledge, how they emerge and interact, I indicated them in italicized font in the following analysis. In this analysis, I identified the occurrence of the strand by its name, and I italicized the name every time it occurred to avoid confusion. At the end, I summarized the insights that emerged from examining my teacher educator knowledge during the planning of an online course.

The pattern of our planning followed a flow of mapping the schedule, articulating the purposes, and interrogating our pedagogical decisions. It would appear at first glance that we began by making a list of tasks, but on closer inspection, we operated out of a backward design approach. According to backward design (Wiggins & McTighe, 2005), planning begins by outlining the desired results and then matching the learning experiences with the desired outcome. Underlying our conversation was a shared commitment to enacting sociocultural theory, modeling for students how they ought to work with English learners, and the need to move the content students were learning from textbook knowledge to content knowledge (*Theory; Content*). When making decisions about my time-honored assignments such as the jigsaw reading, I noticed it was difficult at first for me to let go of it, but that when I verbally restated the desired outcomes of the course, it was easier to set it aside, in a spirit of good, better, best. Thus, issues of *Pedagogical Intent* and *Fixed and Fluid Elements* began being addressed immediately as I grappled with decisions related to *Content Knowledge*.

In a similar vein of prioritizing activities, we had to use restraint in what we planned to ask students to do, always keeping focused on the course goals and the *Milieu* of the course. *Knowledge of Milieu* came into play as I carefully considered what content and learning experiences would be of most benefit to students in this unusual teaching environment and how much time I could expect them to spend given the credit value of the course. I also realized that this kind of thinking and concern had been present in our original construction of the course when it was in person and was already resident in the design for that earlier version.

EXPLORING TEACHER EDUCATOR KNOWLEDGE 69

Both Stefinee and I had experience using online affordances for both synchronous and asynchronous types of learning activities. Even in in-person classes, our course regularly required students to engage with technologies, including teacher observations of video case studies, presenting with PowerPoint, Kahoot quizzes, as well as whatever technologies preservice teachers incorporated in their activity centers for the final projects. Given our experience and also interest in trying out online pedagogies, I felt the need to be careful not to add "bells and whistles," just because we could and instead adjust some of those bells and whistles to better promote the *Pedagogical Intent* of a particular activity.

This caution played out in the discussion about whether to add an online discussion board assignment. Because of a commitment to building relationships (*Value and Fragility of Relationships*) and commitment to sociocultural theory (*Theory*), we wanted more opportunities to hear student voices, but I also knew that such an activity may take the focus away from students working on their activities in their groups. We decided instead to assess their ongoing thinking and learning more informally using a whole class reporting at the beginning of sessions, which we named a Shower of Ideas, and at the last half of every session, by joining small group discussions in the breakout rooms. This thinking led us to understand knowledge teacher educators hold about student-to-student *Relationships* and how working together they could expand their own understanding of *Content* in purposeful ways in this online environment just as our work in in-person environments did.

My analysis of the Planning Vignette is not meant to suggest a specific list of what works and what doesn't work while planning an online course. Rather, the vignette revealed a pattern of discourse that led us to re-examine the purposes of the course. Also, by using backward design, we were able to articulate our *Pedagogical Intent* for the learning experiences leading up to the final project. This allowed us to attend to both what was vital in terms of *Content Knowledge* and how to respond appropriately to what we knew of *Preservice Teacher Knowledge and Belief.*

I made decisions about formal and informal assessments, trying to gauge how to give students just enough support, at just the right moment in their progress in their projects, using formative assessments such as whole class reporting in a Shower of Ideas and frequent check-ins with breakout rooms (*Content Knowledge*). Other examples of flexibility (*Fixed and Fluid Elements*) include the WIP template, which was given to students as a way to collaboratively collect the knowledge they would need as they completed their final project. As Stefinee said, "This is just another way for students to document as they go along and for us to be able to check whether we have provided all the tools for them to draw forward what they know." The WIP was not a required assignment but a helpful framework for organizing the content they were learning in the course and that could be applied in the final project.

The planning stage also involved deciding where to add the *Fixed and Fluid Elements* of the course, including homework, in-class activities, major assignment descriptions and rubrics, due dates, and reserving ample chunks of group work time. In the vignette, I addressed this when I said, "I think one of our obligations is to try to reduce anxiety for them by showing them all the pieces of the final assignment all in one place, right at the start." In the shift to teaching online, I wanted to attend to all of the elements that need to be in place for students to be able to engage flexibly and for teachers to be able to utilize the resources, the timeline, and the group work in flexible ways.

In order to make pedagogical decisions, I observed that we often needed to express our ideas about *Theory*. Stefinee said, "I'm really concerned about how we are going to be responsive and sociocultural online." During planning, while we did not often explicitly refer to theories of design and learning, it became clear as we made decisions about activities and content that theory was guiding our decision-making in implicit ways. For example, my past history teaching this course gave me familiarity with pedagogies based in social theories of learning and communities of practice. The course is designed around Vygotskian principles that learning occurs in interactions, and that for English learners, engaging in reading, writing, listening, and speaking develops cognitive understandings of both content and language. Thus, my heightened concern for *Fixed and Fluid Elements, Pedagogical Intent*, while attending to *Milieu* and *Content* in a project-based course design, was driven by an acknowledgement that these elements must be attended to for optimal interactions and learning to occur.

I recognized in planning my fundamental belief that pedagogy based in sociocultural theory is important, even crucial, to the success of English learners. Because the course is about preparing teachers to instruct English learners using sociocultural theory, frequently within a general education classroom, I am committed to model what sociocultural pedagogy looks like for preservice teachers. This is revealed when Stefinee said, "This is about preservice teachers having time to develop their knowledge of working with English learners." And also, later, when I said, "Each activity needs to support preservice teachers." From my past experience as an adjunct instructor, I also knew that preservice teachers are not accustomed to student-centered, project-based, sociocultural classroom learning at the university. Yet, in planning, I spent a significant amount of time attending to these issues in order to be true to my guiding theoretical principles – not only attending to sociocultural theory but also engaging preservice teachers in learning content using the things they needed to learn in teaching content to English learners (*Preservice Teacher Knowledge and Belief*).

In the 10 sessions of this course on integrating content with language and literacy, an overarching, global concern is how to move preservice teachers' propositional knowledge about English learners into knowledge they can apply as curriculum-makers (*Preservice Teacher Knowledge and Belief; Theory Matters*). Related to this theoretical belief, we stated that we want to "honor our commitment" to sociocultural theory by considering how each learning activity will help us to model and engage in sociocultural pedagogy online. If we had just decided to deliver the content lecture style, we would have been done planning quickly because we already had the content in place.

This questioning of pedagogical practices in order to meet preservice teachers where they are in their learning revealed my knowledge of *Preservice Teacher*

Knowledge and Belief. This strand was expressed in the vignette in our decision to include our TA, Karrie, in our planning meeting and our attention to her comments and contributions. It was also evident when we discussed the class schedule on the learning platform, examined each assignment required, and considered how to make transparent the project-based nature of the course. Since sociocultural teaching is based heavily on trust and building spaces for interaction to take place (*Theory; Relationships*), we took a "less is more" approach to planning. Our concern was evident in reflective statements such as, "If we do this, why?" and "What does this accomplish?" and "We don't want students to have too many tasks." Underlying our discussion and the decisions we made was our deep understanding of the course's *Content* and our *Knowledge of Milieu* (in-person and online).

Also related to *Theory Matters*, there was a stated concern that I meet preservice teachers where they are in their learning. In the vignette, we discussed common myths preservice teachers believe about English learners. Stefinee explained, "You can only learn what you are ready to learn." In this way, a theoretical commitment to sociocultural learning in planning helped me address *Preservice Teacher Knowledge and Belief*, accepting that preservice teachers enter our course with varying backgrounds. When I said, "Every student is different," I am referring to these preservice teachers as well as to the K-12 children they will someday teach.

Knowledge of *Theory* and *Content* also was revealed as we discussed learning experiences that had long been used when teaching the course in person. In other words, by giving up a reading and jigsaw activity, we opened more time in the session "to allow students more time to engage with each other on activities and homework that week." This quote from the vignette highlights a position I held that in order for preservice teachers' textbook-based knowledge to become practical knowledge that would guide their classroom practice, they needed lots of experience integrating knowledge of the content with their experiences, beliefs, and understandings of teaching.

A commitment to sociocultural learning and development of embodied knowledge was revealed in discussions of *Pedagogical Intent*, since from this theoretical stance, learning is developed in interacting with others in a community of practice and is shared using language. We made careful decisions about activities not only so preservice teachers would "have time" and learn from each other but also to model to them the importance of giving their future students time and opportunity to use language and build the learning together. As the Planning Vignette revealed, my understandings about *Theory* and *Content* obviously translate into pedagogical choices in practice. I knew that activities such as a shared reading jigsaw or an online discussion board were potentially valuable learning activities, but in this context, those activities gave way to a commitment to sociocultural learning and a desire for students to have more space to collaborate and develop practical knowledge for teaching English learners outside of direct practice in a classroom.

In the process of examining each assignment, I noticed a tension between what parts of the course design could be fixed and what parts could remain open or fluid (*Fixed and Fluid Elements*). Speaking of this process, I said, "We can spend this time on the details, really questioning the course purposes and design." If we had built in the online discussion board task, this would be a "fixed" element in the course design, with directions easy to post in advance, easy for students to carry out asynchronously, and easy to quickly skim or respond to on our own time as instructors. Fixed elements take some of the uncertainty out of teaching. However, by choosing to rely on breakout rooms for informal assessments, our purpose remained the same but without adding an additional task for students. I already knew that in any course design, in person or online, there is a risk to teach too much content, too quickly, and overwhelm students with moving parts when the intent was only to provide collaborative, engaging activities (*Content Knowledge; Pedagogical Intent*).

In the vignette, I talked about obligations to students and their obligations as well. In my previous work developing an online course, I saw how each activity built on each activity. With every activity and choice mapped, designed, and visible from the very beginning, it became imperative to be aware of *Pedagogical Intent*. I understood that *Pedagogical Intent* begins with understanding the desired outcomes but is not directly tied to observable behavior (like content objectives). Instead, it is very focused at the design level and becomes even more important when preparing online courses, as decisions about fixed elements are being made. In this way, *Pedagogical Intent* was revealed to be intrinsically connected to the other areas of teacher educator knowledge, especially choices in *Content*, an awareness of *Milieu*, and decisions regarding *Fixed and Fluid Elements*.

These planning sessions negotiating the *Fixed and Fluid Elements* of the course led to us wanting to structure class so that it had the same format each time. In the past, class sessions were very different, some being really content-heavy, filled with lots of reading, discussion, and activities, and other sessions given over as student work sessions. It became clear to me during planning that in some ways, when teaching the in-person course, I had been holding to "favorite" assignments based in *Content Knowledge*. In an environment impacted by the COVID-19 pandemic, our students had gone home to their permanent addresses, and the usual patterns of school and work had been interrupted. While in the past, we had not worried about this variability so much in our in-person teaching, in this online context and given my understanding of the importance of *Milieu*, we decided that students might appreciate it if each session followed a predictable pattern. In the vignette, we attended to this concern and made changes in the pattern of class time in order to "make it explicit" and "reduce anxiety" so students might take "creative risks."

These planning discussions led us to develop a new way of organizing the final assignment. In the past, students in small groups gathered the pieces of their curriculum-making and worked together however they wanted to manage it. This time, we provided a template on Google Docs we called their WIP that each group could use as an outline and to which each group member could contribute throughout the course. The suggestion came from our TA but was designed using my previous *Content Knowledge* about backward design learned from Joyce

EXPLORING TEACHER EDUCATOR KNOWLEDGE 73

Nelson in my teacher education program, and that Stefinee had gained in her experiences on the architecture of a classroom.

My account of creating the WIP also revealed our knowledge of *Preservice Teacher Knowledge and Belief* and *Value of Relationships*. With a preservice teacher as a member of our planning conversations, Stefinee often expressed her appreciation to Karrie for her insights and valuable input in course decisions. Indeed, I designed the WIP because of a suggestion Karrie made. She shared how when she took the course, her group had made a shared document to store their ideas, research references, and activities throughout the course. We made this template available for students, hoping that it might alleviate confusion in project planning, but we also allowed for groups to decide for themselves if it would be a useful tool or not. Even more, for this online setting, we reduced the group size from five to three in order to give small groups even more time to talk and collaborate.

In this new teaching context online, I recognized a difference between planning for emergency remote teaching many were rushed to do in the spring of 2020 and the deliberate online pedagogy that Stefinee and I prepared for teaching this course. At one point, I said, "I am sorry the students had to go home for spring term. But honestly, we were already poised to move this course into an online format so hey, it feels like a bonus that we can spend this time on the details, really questioning the course purposes and design." Because of our previous experience in developing courses and moving them online, during this shift to teaching online, we were able to carefully examine our *Knowledge of Content*, adapt our course activities to a new setting (*Knowledge of Milieu*), and attempt to get at what was fundamental, thus avoiding a "frantic frenzy at the beginning of class."

Summary of Teacher Educator Knowledge in Planning

In summary, my teacher educator knowledge was represented as seven strands: *Content Knowledge, Fixed and Flexible Elements, Knowledge of Milieu, Pedagogical Intent, Preservice Teacher Knowledge and Belief, Relationships,* and *Theory.* These seven strands began to take form from the very beginning and were revealed in the ongoing analysis of taking field notes, engaging with a critical friend, composing the vignette, and analyzing the vignette. While all seven strands of teacher educator knowledge were present in the process of planning the course, some strands were more evident than others.

(1) *Content Knowledge.* This strand refers to the decisions I made in planning that emerged from my expertise in the subject matter as well as a professional understanding of how to engage learners with the subject matter (Shulman, 1986). Subject matter was not often explicitly addressed but was definitely present during planning because I was already very familiar with the content of the course. Decisions about content were not as prevalent in the data since we had already made many of these decisions when we designed this course for an in-person format. At one point in the planning, Stefinee and I had

immediate consensus on the content and the pedagogic activity to be addressed. We were startled because we hadn't discussed it. We realized it was our implicit knowledge of content and pedagogy and our commitment to sociocultural theory that guided that decision. This implicit knowledge and belief was always present in any decision we made. Since I had ample prior experience and instruction as an adjunct instructor of preservice teachers, knowledge of pedagogical practices such as project-based learning was also present in planning. Content knowledge informed and enriched other strands including pedagogical intent, fixed and fluid elements, preservice teacher knowledge and beliefs, and relationships.

(2) *Knowledge of Fixed and Fluid Elements.* This refers to the elements of course design that are set in place during planning and areas that are left more flexible. This knowledge was addressed explicitly in planning, especially in relation to decisions about content, activities, and pedagogical intent and the constraints of milieu. In planning to teach a course I had already taught and helped reconstruct many times, this knowledge was challenged often as we discussed how various "favorite" activities would now be engaged in by students online and to make "all the tools" accessible to students. During planning, I worked to make the activities and purposes of the class "explicit" and "methodical." Thus, this strand was informed by and interacted often my knowledge of content, milieu, theory, and pedagogical intent.

(3) *Knowledge of Milieu.* This refers to my understanding that teachers and learners interact with the content in a given milieu, taken from Schwab's (1973) conception of the commonplaces of an educational setting. In planning, this knowledge of milieu was evident in my awareness of the challenges all were facing from the pandemic and because of previous experience designing courses and considering content to be included in online courses. Despite being intimately familiar with the content of the course, my co-teacher and I set aside ample planning space because we were urgently considering what adjustments we would need to make for teaching online. While preparing for the course, I was constantly attending to the settings and environments of learners and teachers in relation to the other strands of teacher educator knowledge. In particular, I was aware of milieu when choosing content and preparing to make resources digitally available, when creating the course activities and identifying pedagogical intent.

(4) *Knowledge of Pedagogical Intent.* This refers to the endeavor of a course designer to identify the intended learning experience desired and align the content delivery and the learning activity accordingly (Allman & Pinnegar, 2020). During the planning of this course, my understanding of pedagogical intent informed the selection of content and even the reduction of required subject matter, the design of activities around carefully targeted goals, the choice of digital tools, and the decision to use a fairly standard format and routine for the course sessions. Given the distress and unusual situation that every student was experiencing, I understood even more the need to prioritize and evaluate learning activities in order to reduce clutter and student anxiety and increase opportunities for students to collaborate on their curriculum

projects. By attending carefully to the pedagogical intent of each learning experience, we kept our focus on our knowledge of preservice teacher learning and the role of a teacher educator in moving their knowledge forward. Therefore, this strand was immediately relevant for the planning of this online course and strongly connected to decisions related to content, theory, milieu, preservice teacher knowledge and beliefs, the value of relationships, and fixed and fluid elements.

(5) *Preservice Teacher Knowledge and Belief.* This refers to the personal practical knowledge of teachers, specifically, a recognition that preservice teachers know a lot about teaching, and my role as a teacher educator is to help shape and reshape the knowledge they already have (Clandinin, 2000). This knowledge was explicitly discussed in the vignette several times, such as when we made decisions about the schedule, developed the WIP template according to our TA's suggestion and input, and considered what preservice teachers already knew about English learners. Even though I had not yet met the preservice teachers I would be teaching, I still made decisions about course design based in my past experience preparing preservice teachers and based on a stated commitment to support and engage preservice teachers in whatever way they are ready to learn. This strand was often entwined with knowledge of relationships and theory.

(6) *Value and Fragility of Relationships.* This refers to the socio-relational course design as an-evidence-based pedagogy for supporting preservice teacher learning and for supporting English learners in developing literacy and language. This strand also refers to the knowledge I hold as a teacher educator about honoring my obligations to students, communicating expectations, and inviting trust. During planning, my knowledge about relationships was more implied than explicit and especially related to matters of theory. In planning, I was thinking ahead about how to help relationships flourish by my careful consideration of an online format, giving more time for groups to work together, reducing the complexity and "busy-ness" of the sessions, and articulating the core expectations for each activity. Thus, even though no relationships with students were developing yet, during planning, my knowledge of and commitment to building relationships still informs and connects with all the strands of content, milieu, theory, preservice teacher knowledge and belief, pedagogical intent, and fixed and fluid elements.

(7) *Knowledge of Theory.* This refers to understandings about the nature of knowledge and how learning occurs. This strand specifically emerged several times in the Planning Vignette, such as a stated commitment to learning as a sociocultural act, moving textbook knowledge into practical knowledge, and engaging preservice teachers in theory-based practices for English learners. Much of the time, knowledge of theory was implicitly enacted in connection with other strands such as when we made decisions related to pedagogy, content, technology, and student engagement. From the project-based course design to the reduced size of groups in breakout rooms, these decisions about how to set up the learning environment cannot be separated from a strong underlying strand of theoretical knowledge.

WHAT DOES THE TEACHING VIGNETTE REVEAL ABOUT TEACHER EDUCATOR KNOWLEDGE?

ABSTRACT

The strands of teacher educator knowledge are explained using an analytic narrative vignette to represent data collected during the teaching of an online course in the spring of 2020. The Teaching Vignette represents examples of the teaching experiences I was engaged in for an undergraduate class for pre-service teachers to learn Content-Based Instruction in Language and Literacy for teaching English language learners. In the vignette, the two instructors taught and managed sessions of the course from their laptops together at the same table. The preservice teachers participated via Zoom. The Teaching Vignette was analyzed systematically by highlighting the strands of teacher educator knowledge as they appeared and noting, when evident, how they interrelated with each other. In this way, I showed how the strands of teacher educator knowledge became more visible during the teaching of the course. In addition, I discussed how the strands are interrelated and connected to each other. After the analysis, I explain the insights that emerged from examining my teacher educator knowledge during the teaching stage by considering each of the seven strands of teacher educator knowledge.

Keywords: Teacher educator knowledge; TESOL K-12; online teacher education; analytic narrative vignettes; exemplars; teacher education; pedagogical content knowledge; teacher knowledge; preservice teachers; pedagogical intent

In this study, three analytic narrative vignettes serve to represent how the strands of teacher educator knowledge were evident from the beginning in the process of course design, during the teaching of the course, and after teaching in the process of evaluating and reflecting on course outcomes. In the last chapter, the Planning Vignette was analyzed for insights into teacher educator knowledge. In this chapter, the Teaching Vignette highlights how the strands of teacher educator

---

Exploring Teacher Educator Knowledge
Advances in Research on Teaching, Volume 48, 77–89
Copyright © 2025 Celina Dulude Lay
Published under exclusive licence by Emerald Publishing Limited
ISSN: 1479-3687/doi:10.1108/S1479-368720240000048006

knowledge were revealed and how they entwined and informed each other while teaching the course online. In the next chapter, the Reflecting Vignette captures how these strands of teacher educator knowledge were represented in my actions and thinking beyond the teaching and planning.

Each of the three vignettes is intended to capture the major understandings about teacher educator knowledge but not necessarily include every example from the field texts, simply those that provided the strongest evidence. Again, these major understandings are represented as seven strands of teacher educator knowledge, evident in each narrative vignette. The seven strands are: *Content Knowledge, Fixed and Fluid Elements, Knowledge of Milieu, Pedagogical Intent, Preservice Teacher Knowledge and Belief, Value and Fragility of Relationships,* and *Theory Matters.* For reference, brief definitions and theoretical foundations of the seven strands are listed below:

Descriptions of Strands of Teacher Educator Knowledge

Content Knowledge	Associated with Shulman's work on pedagogical content knowledge, the expertise a teacher educator holds on subject matter as well as the professional understanding of how to engage learners with the subject matter. Also emerging from Schwab's conception of the commonplaces of an educational setting, that teachers and learners interact with the content in a given milieu (Craig, 2008; Schwab, 1973).
Fixed and Fluid Elements	There are elements of a course design that can be set and fixed and others that can vary. Decisions about what to fix and what to allow to vary reveal the theoretical underpinnings of a course designer and purposes of a course.
Knowledge of Milieu	Also related to Schwab's work, in curriculum design, the milieu is important to consider along with the teacher, the student, and the subject matter. Indeed, attending to the settings and environments of learners and teachers becomes just as integral to curriculum-making as subject matter expertise.
Pedagogical Intent	A term taken from Allman and Pinnegar's (2020) research. Identifying pedagogical intent is an endeavor of a teacher educator to align competing goals of delivery of content and teaching practice. Teacher educators target an intended *learning experience* hoped to be accomplished when assigning a learning task, thus informing the selection of content, activities, and, if designing online, digital tools.
Preservice Teacher Knowledge and Belief	Associated with Clandinin's (2000) assertions about teachers' personal practical knowledge, this knowledge comes from a recognition that preservice teachers know a lot about teaching, and a teacher educator's role is to help shape and reshape the knowledge they already have. Teacher educators identify those teacher education practices particularly attuned to supporting changes and growth in preservice teacher knowledge and belief.
Value and Fragility of Relationships	In a socio-relational course design now shifted to an online format, knowledge a teacher educator may hold for developing teacher–student relationships, and especially for supporting student learning communities.
Theory Matters	A recognition that theory underlies and drives a teacher educator's decisions related to pedagogy, content, technology, and relationships. In unpacking, understandings about the nature of knowledge and how learning occurs in educational environments emerge.

The strands of teacher educator knowledge pervaded the data during planning and especially during teaching. While teaching the course, the data revealed my nuanced and connected understanding of the strands, represented in the vignette.

TEACHING

The Teaching Vignette captured exemplars of the kind of teaching experiences I was engaged in during a spring class in 2020 and revealed the strands of teacher educator knowledge that emerged in analysis of the data related to teaching the course. Following the vignette, I emphasize how teacher educator knowledge that is drawn on in-person teaching emerged, changed, or deepened in the shift to teaching online. In both composing the vignettes and unpacking their meaning, I attend to teacher educator knowledge that already existed in my thinking as a teacher educator that was then revealed as the teaching context shifted. I conclude the analysis with a summary of how each of the strands of teacher educator knowledge was revealed in both explicit and implicit ways and how they influenced each other in each phase of planning, teaching, and reflecting on the course.

Teaching Vignette: Teaching Content-Based Literacy and Language Instruction Online

In our first session of class, Dr Pinnegar introduced herself by sharing where she grew up in St George, Utah. "It's important in our learning to find connections with each other. Even though we are on Zoom, we are going to have lots of opportunities to interact. Relationships in education are the most important thing... These people in this room are going to be some of your best support as you take up teaching."

While she talked, I tried to memorize each of the 15 faces and names showing up Brady-Bunch style on my screen. When it was my turn, I reiterated the importance of relationships, sharing how Dr Pinnegar had been my professor as a preservice teacher.

"We're hoping we will be willing to laugh at each other in kind ways as we work out an online class. Dr. Pinnegar, and through her, me, since she was my teacher at BYU, are very committed to sociocultural learning as an evidence-based practice for English learners to develop language and literacy. So, in everything that we thought about for this class, we are thinking about how we can make the relationships matter and how we can engage you in learning this content in the same way we want you to work with your students."

Then, we spent some time outlining the course and assigning groups. I kept my eye on the clock. Dr Pinnegar said, "Our main concern when we decided to put students in the same group for all the assignments was to simplify the amount of coordinating you would have to do for presentations and then later for final curriculum projects. Usually when you do your group's presentation, we let you do whatever you want, but to simplify it we have given you specific directions.

But please read that assignment carefully and if you have suggestions for adjustment let us know."

I jumped in, "Yes, the class will go fast – twice a week, five weeks, and we're done. Because of that, you need to let us know if something is not working."

Even though we made this explicit, we knew we would have to worry about this decision and watch the small groups of three carefully week by week. We also knew that while we had built typical safeguards into the assignments to reduce group members taking advantage of each other, I was always hyper-aware of group interactions. That day, like other days, we moved from breakout room to breakout room, observing how the groups functioned together, communicated with each other and delegated tasks appropriately. We would join groups and then the two of us would meet in the main Zoom room for a few minutes to confer about what was happening and if there was any confusion or concern we needed to fix.

For the second session, we had asked students to look over the timeline and ask questions about the assignments. We wanted students to see that we took their questions, their concerns seriously, because we knew that we would always need to nourish relationships, and this was one way to do it. In this second class, one student pointed out discrepancies in due dates. "Thank you for pointing this out," I said. Then, on the spot and with students waiting, I cleaned up those mistakes. Another student immediately asked us to clarify directions. Our responsiveness seemed to make them more open in expressing confusion or point out what they perceived as our errors.

We usually began class by inviting every student to offer an insight or a question about what they were learning from the homework. Students engaged enthusiastically in this routine activity. We called this activity a Shower of Ideas. One day, we used the activity as a quiz after a guest teacher expert visited via Zoom to teach the students about using Sheltered Instruction Observation Protocol (SIOP). After the guest presentation, I asked, "You have a colleague without an ESL endorsement who has several English learners in her class. She asks you for advice. What are the big ideas from SIOP that you will share?"

After some silence, one student responded, taking up the role play invitation, "Your English learners are capable of being held to high academic standards. Let me tell you about comprehensible input. . ."

Another student added, "These are some ways I assess if students understand the concept, even if they are limited in English. I can show you how I do it."

One day, we both had positive experiences visiting with groups. During the breakout sessions, I joined one group to listen in and offer help. After briefly acknowledging me with a hello, they immediately went back to their project. Corinne described her progress on her activity but then eagerly added, "Dani, I saw this link and thought it would be so perfect for you. See this?" Corinne then shared her screen and showed her group what she had found. They all exclaimed and started brainstorming how to incorporate these new ideas into their overarching objectives for their activity centers. Meanwhile, Dr Pinnegar was visiting with another group, amazed at their camaraderie. She asked them if they had known each other before. They all shook their heads no.

EXPLORING TEACHER EDUCATOR KNOWLEDGE

Roxanne asked, "How did you decide to put us in these groups? I didn't even know these women before, but I love collaborating with them. These are my new best friends."

In the final sessions, I observed groups working with smooth efficiency to finish their projects. One group was chatting about an upcoming wedding when I joined. They were aware I was there, and it only took a moment before Jane said, "Celina, glad you're here. We have some questions for you, but I had to tell my group, these last few months have been so hard."

I was amused. "Oh, why is that? Being away from your fiancé?"

"No, it's all about the dress! I haven't had any bread for EIGHT WEEKS!"

They all laughed and then immediately segued into their questions.

"Celina, when we write our directions to the activities, we want to include pictures. Is that what you mean by providing text modification?"

"Yes, that's great. Show me."

"See, we have pictures of what the kids should do at each table. The picture along with the text can help struggling readers and English learners know what to do at this center."

"Exactly. Let me know if you have any more questions. Looking good. And Jane, so excited for your upcoming wedding."

Analysis of the Teaching Vignette

Just like in reporting the analysis of the previous vignette on planning, I analyzed the Teaching Vignette systematically by highlighting the seven strands of teacher educator knowledge as they unfolded and connected, and I indicated them in italicized font to provide emphasis and clarity. However, where, when, and how these strands of teacher educator knowledge were present and intertwined in the Teaching Vignette was not identical to the ways in which they were present in the Planning Vignette. Therefore, presenting the Teaching Vignette and presenting analysis of the strands in the context of teaching expands understanding of them. Again, these strands of teacher educator knowledge are: *Content Knowledge, Fixed and Fluid Elements, Knowledge of Milieu, Pedagogical Intent, Preservice Teacher Knowledge and Belief, Value and Fragility of Relationships,* and *Theory Matters*. At the end, I summarized the insights that emerged from examining my teacher educator knowledge while teaching this online course.

Unlike my raw notes from planning and reflecting, the records of teaching were mostly taken from recordings of the whole class portions of Zoom meetings. I was uncomfortable watching myself in the Zoom recording, especially in the first minutes of the first session as I introduced myself to the class. While Dr Pinnegar sounded confident and comfortable, to myself, I sounded a bit too self-conscious and ingratiating. If I were a student watching me (I thought), I would think that teacher was mildly interesting, a little milquetoast, or worst of all, irritating. However, once I got past the discomfort of watching myself, I was able to consider what the teaching interaction revealed to me about my teacher educator knowledge, and I was immediately reminded of the *Value and Fragility of Relationships*. As a teacher educator, I knew that relationships between preservice teachers and teacher educators could be disrupted simply because of perceptions, first impressions, or misunderstandings that could make it difficult for students to connect to, engage with, and value what the teacher educator is offering.

Indeed, this strand about the *Value and Fragility of Relationships* immediately came to the forefront in the Teaching Vignette. Now that teaching the course was in motion, "I tried to memorize each of the fifteen faces and names showing up Brady-Bunch style on my screen." Dr Pinnegar told the class, "Relationships in education are the most important thing." In class introductions, in the very first minutes of the course, we "reiterated the importance of relationships" and explained how "we are very committed to sociocultural learning as an evidence-based practice for English learners to develop language and literacy" (*Content; Theory*). I encouraged students to notice how the class was designed for "learning this content in the same way we want you to work with your students" (*Content; Theory*).

Theoretical knowledge, especially a stance that learning occurs as a social process, was continually evident in practice and not just word, in both Dr Pinnegar's and my engagement in pacing, encouraging, and allowing student participation. For example, checking in on breakout groups was a tricky business. In the vignette, I assessed the health and progress of groups, ready to intervene or make adjustments if necessary. As I joined a breakout room, I was always immediately aware of the climate – whether it was positive and productive (*Milieu*). Further, I was very aware that I had multiple responsibilities, such as: was *Content* being accurately represented and applied, was the activity meeting its *Pedagogical Intent*, were the preservice teachers working together with all participants contributing and learning. This kind of attention to how well groups were collaborating is evidence of both an attention to *Theory*, especially sociocultural pedagogy, and *Relationships*.

Just like when a teacher drifts from table to table in a classroom, it was often a struggle to determine accurately what each group needed when it was their turn for a visit from me. For example, when joining a breakout room, I could potentially make the assumption that a group is off task, such as when I joined the group in the Teaching Vignette who were discussing wedding plans, and come in with a heavy-handed presence. In this exemplar, I described myself as silently standing by, knowing they could see that I was there, willing to observe and hear the group converse. Fortunately, I resisted pushing them toward a focus on the *Content* or their engagement with the *Fixed Elements* to be considered.

As it turned out, this group had progressed already very far in their planning, as revealed when they "immediately segued into their questions." Although they were not waiting for a teacher's help, they were taking a moment from what had obviously been a deep engagement with the assignment to chat. They were not embarrassed to be caught off task, and truly, there was no reason for them to be. As their teacher educator, I was glad that they were enjoying their time together. From the questions they asked me, it appeared they were producing strong activity centers (*Pedagogical Intent; Content*).

EXPLORING TEACHER EDUCATOR KNOWLEDGE

In the past, I have had students tell me cheerfully that they have no questions and everything is great, and then during final grading, I would find out their final projects were not very high quality. Because of this past experience, in the vignette, even as I described the positive experiences and groups "working with smooth efficiency," I was not seduced into believing that the amiable hard-working atmosphere I typically experienced in the breakout rooms was the whole story (*Preservice Teacher Knowledge and Belief*). Also, from such encounters, I have learned to pause and listen when I join groups, as I did here, in order to observe what is really going on.

More strands of teacher educator knowledge were evident in the story about the wedding dress, and it was not about the dress. When I joined this group, Jane asked, "Celina, when we write our directions to the activities, we want to include pictures. Is that what you mean by providing text modification?" In Jane's question to me and subsequent explanation of her activity design, she showed me that she was comfortable using the language and concepts of the course, easily conversing about text modifications and appropriate design for supporting the academic development of English learners (*Content Knowledge, Pedagogical Intent*). In preparing to teach the course, it was important to me to build in ample space for preservice teachers to express their growing skill in speaking the language of teaching (*Preservice Teacher Knowledge and Belief*), and now, while teaching, in this time reserved for groups to work, I was able to observe preservice teachers using the academic discourse of teaching language learners and support their thinking through dialogue (*Fixed and Fluid Elements*). In action, my teaching was often purposeful as I tried to model effective sociocultural peda-gogical practices in the hope that these future teachers will also allow their English learners space and time to explore, try out new academic words, clarify, and explain the academic concepts they are learning (*Theory*).

Although assignments were fixed during planning, I knew certain details and adjustments would need to be addressed in the moment (*Fixed and Fluid Ele-ments*). In this class, students in breakout groups often had a question that I could either answer immediately, draw from a group member, or track down an answer while the group continued working (*Preservice Teacher Knowledge and Belief, Content Knowledge*). In an in-person environment, co-teachers' interactions are generally always public, but in a Zoom classroom, Dr Pinnegar and I could quickly confer in private when we met in between checking on breakout rooms or directly messaging each other or the TA. In these moments, we attended to whether the *Content* was being taken up, whether the *Pedagogical Intent* of the activity was being met, whether *Preservice Teacher Knowledge* was being built, and whether the *Relationships* in the groups were thriving. Using breakout rooms created a valuable space where students could build their knowledge because they could speak freely with each other without having to worry about being too loud, overheard, or recorded (*Content Knowledge, Pedagogical Intent, Preservice Teacher Knowledge and Beliefs*). In this format, they knew everyone would be able to speak and speak freely with each other, unlike in a whole class discussion or lecture where students' opportunities to express their ideas is limited

(*Pedagogical Intent*). These were affordances that I recognized in this new online teaching environment that now added to my knowledge of *Milieu*.

The Teaching Vignette revealed the tentative nature of teacher–student relationships, such as during the role-play quiz at the end of a guest speaker visit (*Value and Fragility of Relationships*). In this scenario, I asked students to respond to the question about how to help a colleague who had some questions about an English learner. Although responses did not flow from the students immediately, when they finally spoke, they revealed their familiarity and comfort with the language of the course, addressing concepts such as "comprehensible input" and assessments for students with limited English vocabulary (*Content; Pedagogical Intent*). However, unlike past, more enthusiastic experiences with students sharing their ideas in our routine Shower of Ideas at the beginning of each class, this time, there was a distinct pause and hesitation before students began to participate (*Preservice Teacher Knowledge and Belief*). The students showed reluctance to participate when the familiar Shower of Ideas format was now being used as a summative quiz, instead of as a more comfortable and informal beginning-of-class discussion (*Pedagogical Intent*). Student preheld beliefs about being tested may have hindered their willingness to participate (*Preservice Teacher Knowledge and Beliefs*).

Also revealed in the vignette was how we as teacher educators made ongoing decisions regarding *Pedagogical Intent* that were founded in *Theory*. Indeed, the vignette revealed during our frequent visits to small groups that the learning purposes of the project-based curriculum activity were being met, and students' learning was proceeding as desired. While teaching, I often found myself attuned to the pacing and time spent on each activity. This awareness of time is typical for any experienced teacher, but particularly true in order for me to be true to my guiding goals for this course. In the vignette, awareness of pacing and time was revealed in the proportion of the vignette devoted to whole class time compared to the number of exemplars that revealed small group engagement. The vignette made clear that during teaching, I allowed time and space for groups to be able to develop their ideas for their final projects, listened to students articulate their personal practical knowledge of teaching English learners, and modeled a commitment to sociocultural learning with dedicated class time (*Milieu, Preservice Teacher Knowledge and Belief, Content*).

The vignette revealed that much of the time I spent in class looked more like management of the various pieces and definitely was not a one-sided delivery of content that would have occurred with a lecture format. This reflected my previous understanding of how *Fixed and Fluid Elements* needed to come together in productive ways in order for student learning to flourish. For me, this understanding was deepened as I taught alongside Dr Pinnegar and observed her ways of conveying a willingness to listen and be flexible. For example, when explaining presentations, Dr Pinnegar said, "If you have suggestions for adjustment let us know." Even with established *Content, Fixed Elements*, and other parameters, this openness to student need and response (*Fluid Elements*) revealed a commitment to the pedagogical demands of sociocultural *Theory*. In the vignette, I was often busy addressing student questions related to the development of materials, presentations, and assignments, keeping the class activities moving according to schedule, and supporting groups in their breakout rooms during the last portion of each session (*Milieu, Preservice Teacher Knowledge and Belief, Relationships*). My responses attempted to convey this same openness I observed in Dr Pinnegar, such as when I said, "Thank you for pointing this out." Further, as I noted, "Our responsiveness seemed to make them more open." Especially given the context of teaching in an online environment, student questions were one of the most important windows into preservice teacher thinking and also for establishing and supporting teacher–student relationships. Because of this understanding, encouraging student questions and making time and space for them was an imperative in the course. We took measures such as extending the wait time after the Shower of Ideas, asking in break out rooms, being available at the end of the session, and treating questions and comments with respect.

The participation of preservice teachers in the vignette revealed how, by design, much of the speaking and even teaching in the class was being done by them (*Pedagogical Intent, Theory Matters*). In each session, students were engaged at the beginning of class in sharing their insights from readings and homework in a Shower of Ideas. Then, students were engaged in class activities such as presenting to the class on the Standards for Effective Pedagogy, analyzing corpus studies of textbooks, meeting with a guest lecturer, or getting help on their final activity center projects from the mentor teacher for whom they were designing these activity centers. During the final portion of each session, students were engaged with their groups in breakout rooms, designing the various pieces of their activity centers with a focus on building language and literacy in English learners. All of this student engagement was represented in the vignette as students talking, asking, listening, presenting, sharing a screen, writing, and reading. As teacher educators, Dr Pinnegar and I were busy too, but what we did looked like managing, clarifying, attending to the pacing, and deciding when to intervene and when to exercise restraint (*Preservice Teacher Knowledge and Belief, Milieu*).

During teaching, I became more comfortable with my own understanding that sociocultural, project-based learning feels messier and more uncertain to students and that part of my role was to be patient, relax, and patiently answer all those questions, always striving to achieve better clarity next time (*Theory Matters, Fixed and Fluid Elements*). Particularly in this new context of teaching online during a global pandemic, I felt an added obligation to attend to student confusion by designing the course with *Fixed and Flexible Elements*, making sure each activity has been reduced to its essence and pedagogical purpose, and making transparent how these assignments built to the final project. As represented in the Planning Vignette, this work was mainly accomplished in preparing to teach the course. In this teaching phase, the fixed elements were set in motion, referred to often, and adjusted as needed. In the moments of teaching, I attended to this obligation by modeling a relaxed willingness to learn and "nourish relationships" and by taking student questions seriously. After fixing some mistakes in the schedule, I noted, "Our responsiveness seemed to make them more open in expressing confusion or point out what they perceived as our errors."

There is another aspect of the *Value and Fragility of Relationships* worth mentioning in relation to the vignette. I have past experience and knowledge about how tenuous connections built in a learning community can be damaged by students not inclined to take up the invitation to participate in sociocultural learning. I have also been in classes where one student destroyed learning opportunities for group members. This did not occur in this class, but it is clear in statements such as, "I was always hyper-aware of group interactions," and, "We knew we would have to worry ... and watch the small groups of three carefully week by week," that I am aware of the possibility and ready to intervene if needed. I knew that careful attention to how the relationships were functioning would increase the likelihood that the activities would meet their *Pedagogical Intent*.

There are other ways the vignette revealed how students were participants in each other's learning (*Theory Matters*). Perhaps because of time given for students to discuss and plan together in their small groups as well as the readily available materials needed to support learning (*Fluid and Fixed Elements*), there was evidence that group members were particularly aware of the needs of other students, even when working independently. For example, Corinne was eager to share resources she found on her own with a member of her group. She said, "Dani, I saw this link and thought it would be so perfect for you. See this?" After she shared the new ideas with her group, I observed, "They all exclaimed and started brainstorming how to incorporate these new ideas into their overarching objectives for their activity centers." Thus, by attending to the *Value of Relationships* as a matter of *Theory* and making certain that needed materials were present and accessible (*Fixed and Fluid Elements*), I was able to observe positive evidence of preservice teacher learning as they engaged in the learning experiences that had been planned with careful attention to the activity's *Pedagogical Intent*.

Summary of Teacher Educator Knowledge in Teaching

In summary, in the moments of teaching online, the seven strands of teacher educator knowledge were represented: *Content Knowledge, Fixed and Flexible Elements, Knowledge of Milieu, Pedagogical Intent, Preservice Teacher Knowledge and Belief, Value and Fragility of Relationships,* and *Theory.* The strands were revealed throughout analysis of the field data, while composing the vignette, and in unpacking the vignette. While all seven strands of teacher educator knowledge were present while teaching the course, some strands were more evident than others.

(1) *Content Knowledge.* During teaching, content knowledge refers to the subject matter taught and available to preservice teachers as well as my ongoing pedagogical efforts to strengthen, enrich, or support their learning. As I was teaching, preservice teacher knowledge of content was explicitly revealed in their discourse with each other, questions to me, and as they engaged with the class resources. This made visible to me whether they were learning and

EXPLORING TEACHER EDUCATOR KNOWLEDGE

understanding the content that activity was designed to teach them. Schwab's (1973) commonplaces of an educational setting add to my understanding that the content of a curriculum can be tailored according to time and place, teacher and learner. In the vignette on teaching, preservice teachers interacted with content in small-group activities to prepare presentations and design curriculum projects. Significantly, as I reviewed the actions of students during activities, I was reminded of my own knowledge of the subject matter, particularly since I was tracking whether they were learning the content I wanted them to learn. In these interactions as I responded to students, I was reminded that teacher educators require a deep knowledge of the subject matter in order to be ready, in the moment, to adjust, clarify, reteach, and otherwise move preservice teachers forward in their own learning (Shulman, 1986). During the teaching phase, the teacher educator's knowledge of content enhanced other strands including theory, pedagogical intent, fixed and fluid elements, and especially preservice teacher knowledge and beliefs.

(2) *Knowledge of Fixed and Fluid Elements.* This refers to the prepared elements of course design that now are drawn on each class to provide structure and to the action and response of the teacher educator in the moment of instruction. The fluid aspects of this kind of knowledge were evident in the ability of the instructor to foresee and forestall confusion, make in-the-moment adjustments, and allow for flexibility when required. The fixed elements are the materials, directions, and other resources provided to the learners that are already prepared and in place and facilitate the instructor's ability to respond effectively in the moment. The teacher educator's knowledge of fixed and fluid elements was relevant and expressed frequently during teaching. It was especially visible in relation to preservice teacher questions about content, digital availability of resources, schedules, and other documents, as well as in the routine pattern and structure of class time. It was also evident as I made in-flight decisions to alter or adjust activities in the moment of instruction. As I made adjustments, I was reminded how much more difficult that was in an online version of the course than it is face to face. During teaching, it helped to see these elements as an interplay rather than a dichotomy, since both fixed and fluid elements were useful, even necessary, in teaching the course. Since many of the fixed elements were decided upon during planning, they were not as obvious or explicit in teaching except when adjustments needed to be made. Especially in online teaching, I recognized that fixed elements were fundamental for the course to operate smoothly, meet pedagogical intent, and ironically, for adjustments to be made quickly and effectively. As a result, during teaching, attention to this strand interacted often with teacher educator knowledge about content, milieu, and preservice teacher knowledge and belief.

(3) *Knowledge of Milieu.* This strand refers to the importance of the context and other constraints of the environment to the teaching and learning. Given the online format, distant location of each student joining class, and the unusual challenges that every student was experiencing in a global pandemic, I understood even more the need to monitor learning activities, students'

acquisition of content, constantly gauge student anxiety, and support student collaboration on their curriculum projects. One unique aspect of knowledge of milieu in an online context is an understanding of the variability in student access and my own technical knowledge in supporting them. This was often relevant to understanding clearly the fixed and fluid elements. In addition, I was aware of milieu in relation to preservice teacher knowledge and belief, teaching the content, and theory.

(4) *Knowledge of Pedagogical Intent.* This is a concept based on the work of Allman and Pinnegar (2020) that identifies what a teacher educator designs a learning task to accomplish. Attention to pedagogical intent guides a teacher educator in identifying content, developing activities, and in selecting and modifying digital tools. During teaching, this knowledge was relevant as I observed and supported students participating in learning experiences together. Pedagogical intent was prevalent during planning, but now during teaching, it was still relevant as I worked closely alongside students and observed carefully to determine if an activity was working as intended and how to adjust fixed and fluid elements to meet that intent. Pedagogical intent was closely connected with knowledge of milieu, preservice teacher knowledge and belief, theory, and content.

(5) *Preservice Teacher Knowledge and Belief.* During planning, activities are designed, content is selected, often based on the teacher educator's understanding of the knowledge and belief that preservice teachers bring to the course. During teaching, it refers to my understanding that preservice teachers already know a lot about teaching, my commitment to honoring their perspectives, ideas, questions, and growth, and my attention to what they are learning and whether they are able to pull forward their prior knowledge and integrate it. This knowledge was revealed in the vignette when Dr Pinnegar and I interacted with students, helping to shape and reshape the knowledge they already had. This strand was connected to decisions related to milieu, content, theory, and fixed and fluid elements.

(6) *Value and Fragility of Relationships.* This strand constantly weighs on the thinking and action of teacher educators during teaching. I recognized that teacher educators are hyper-sensitive to the responses of students to each other and to the teacher educator. This strand was also represented by my commitment to building class connection and discourse that invited questions and openness in order to support learning. In the act of teaching, my knowledge about relationships was evident when I visited breakout rooms, for example, and made fine-tuned decisions about when and how to engage, listen, question, or redirect which were not always explicit. Goodlad's (1990a) assertion that teachers are valued for their judgment was evident here too, since much of relationship building and communicating well happens quickly, as teacher educators engage with preservice teachers, see a need, and act on it. Because the course ran only 5 weeks and students joined via Zoom, my "hyper-" awareness of the fragility of relationships was heightened during teaching. Teacher educator knowledge of relationships was especially connected to milieu, preservice teacher knowledge and belief, and theory.

EXPLORING TEACHER EDUCATOR KNOWLEDGE

(7) *Knowledge of Theory.* This refers to a theoretical stance about the nature of knowledge and how learning occurs. This strand specifically emerged in my teaching in relation to student engagement in the activities of the course, especially reporting during a Shower of Ideas and collaborating in their small groups to build curriculum for English learners. Much of the time, my knowledge of theory was present in the fixed and fluid elements of the course. The kinds of activities designed and the insistence on interaction with fellow students and application of ideas to specific practice set in place the theories on which this course was constructed. Thus, knowledge of theory was implicitly enacted in connection with other strands, such as when I engaged with students on issues of content, listened to them think and apply their textbook knowledge to the curriculum they were making, and in my efforts to value and strengthen relationships. This strand connected with all the strands, but especially as I engaged with students.

WHAT DOES THE REFLECTING VIGNETTE REVEAL ABOUT TEACHER EDUCATOR KNOWLEDGE?

ABSTRACT

The strands of teacher educator knowledge are explained using an analytic narrative vignette to represent data collected while evaluating the experience of teaching an online course for preservice teachers in the spring of 2020. Because of the worldwide COVID-19 pandemic, it was my first time moving this particular course from in-person to an online format, and there was much to evaluate and wonder about. The Reflecting Vignette represents the data gathered after teaching, including debriefing meetings that occurred with my co-instructor immediately following a class session, as well as final reflections engaged in after the course was completed. For example, in the vignette, I critique some of my decisions, such as rushing through the directions, but also allow myself a measure of grace, where I am able to be patient with glitches or my own shortcomings with technology. In such narrative description, the strands were revealed. At this point in data collection and analysis, the strands were solidified and robust, with analysis occurring in the work of reflection and in unpacking the vignette. This is made clear in the explanation that follows the vignette. After the analysis of the vignette, I explain the insights that emerged from examining the strands during the reflecting and evaluating stage and how the strands were revealed in both explicit and implicit ways.

Keywords: Teacher educator knowledge; preservice teacher knowledge; reflection; pedagogical content knowledge; pedagogical intent; analytic narrative vignettes; exemplars; online teacher education; course design; theory practice divide

Three analytic narrative vignettes were created as exemplars of how seven strands of teacher educator knowledge were evident: before teaching, from beginning the process of course design; during teaching, in the moments and interactions with students and curriculum; and after teaching, in the process of evaluating and

---

Exploring Teacher Educator Knowledge
Advances in Research on Teaching, Volume 48, 91–101
Copyright © 2025 Celina Dulude Lay
Published under exclusive licence by Emerald Publishing Limited
ISSN: 1479-3687/doi:10.1108/S1479-368720240000048007

reflecting on course outcomes. In Chapter 5, the Planning Vignette was explored for insights into teacher educator knowledge. In Chapter 6, the Teaching Vignette represented the teaching experience and how the strands of teacher educator knowledge were revealed. In this chapter, the Reflecting Vignette shows how the strands of teacher educator knowledge were represented in my actions and thinking beyond the teaching and planning.

Each of the three vignettes is intended to represent the major understandings about teacher educator knowledge but not necessarily include every example from the data, simply those that provided the strongest evidence. All seven strands of teacher educator knowledge are represented in each narrative vignette. The seven strands are: *Content Knowledge, Fixed and Fluid Elements, Knowledge of Milieu, Pedagogical Intent, Preservice Teacher Knowledge and Belief, Value and Fragility of Relationships*, and *Theory Matters*. For reference, brief definitions and theoretical foundations of the seven strands are listed below.

Descriptions of Strands of Teacher Educator Knowledge

Content Knowledge	Associated with Shulman's work on pedagogical content knowledge, the expertise a teacher educator holds on subject matter as well as the professional understanding of how to engage learners with the subject matter. Also emerging from Schwab's conception of the commonplaces of an educational setting, that teachers and learners interact with the content in a given milieu (Craig, 2008; Schwab, 1973).
Fixed and Fluid Elements	There are elements of a course design that can be set and fixed, and others that can vary. Decisions about what to fix and what to allow to vary reveal the theoretical underpinnings of a course designer and purposes of a course.
Knowledge of Milieu	Also related to Schwab's work, in curriculum design, the milieu is important to consider along with the teacher, the student, and the subject matter. Indeed, attending to the settings and environments of learners and teachers becomes just as integral to curriculum-making as subject matter expertise.
Pedagogical Intent	A term taken from Allman and Pinnegar's (2020) research. Identifying pedagogical intent is an endeavor of a teacher educator to align competing goals of delivery of content and teaching practice. Teacher educators target an intended *learning experience* hoped to be accomplished when assigning a learning task, thus informing the selection of content, activities, and, if designing online, digital tools.
Preservice Teacher Knowledge and Belief	Associated with Clandinin's (2000) assertions about teachers' personal practical knowledge, this knowledge comes from a recognition that preservice teachers know a lot about teaching, and a teacher educator's role is to help shape and reshape the knowledge they already have. Teacher educators identify those teacher education practices particularly attuned to supporting changes and growth in preservice teacher knowledge and belief.
Value and Fragility of Relationships	In a socio-relational course design now shifted to an online format, knowledge a teacher educator may hold for developing teacher–student relationships, and especially for supporting student learning communities.

EXPLORING TEACHER EDUCATOR KNOWLEDGE   93

(Continued)

Descriptions of Strands of Teacher Educator Knowledge	
Theory Matters	A recognition that theory underlies and drives a teacher educator's decisions related to pedagogy, content, technology, and relationships. In unpacking, understandings about the nature of knowledge and how learning occurs in educational environments emerge.

This analytic narrative vignette captured exemplars of the debriefing and reflecting I engaged in and revealed the strands of teacher educator knowledge that emerged in the analysis of the data related to reflecting on the course.

REFLECTING

The first part of the Reflecting Vignette captures the conversational pattern of an immediate debriefing following a class session. The discussion pattern of the final evaluation meeting, represented in the second portion of the vignette, in turn captured the topics and thinking in a different way and relied on excerpts from my final journaling. After the vignette, I have provided an analysis of the vignette to make visible and clear to the reader evidence of the strands and how my teacher educator knowledge unfolded. I conclude the analysis of the Reflecting Vignette with a summary of how each of the seven strands of teacher educator knowledge were revealed in both explicit and implicit ways and how they influenced each other.

Reflecting Vignette: Reflecting on the Course and My Knowledge

After a synchronous online session, my head was pounding from listening so intently and observing faces so closely and keeping my own face schooled in an expression of engaged interest. I could feel the letdown of teacher-tension as the last student waved goodbye and left the Zoom meeting. Stefinee, the TA, and I stared at each other over Zoom, the online space suddenly much smaller.

"Are you as tired as I am?" Stefinee quipped. The thing about working with Stefinee is that she always speaks honestly and treats each of us, me, the graduate student and Karrie, the undergraduate TA, as valued colleagues.

I managed a grin and then said, honestly, "I always feel wrung out after the first session."

Stefinee said, "As teachers, we tend to be really emotionally 'on,' but it's hard in this context to gauge how class is going. We can't really read their faces as well on Zoom."

"What do you mean?" Karrie had been working as a TA long enough to know that her questions were valued.

Stefinee continued, "You've taught in practicum, Karrie, working one-on-one trying to figure out what a child knows. It takes observation and all your concentration."

Karrie nodded, "Yeah, you're right."

Stefinee explained, "But in Zoom we can't see clearly enough their facial features, the nuances of their body language, the subtlety, yet we are still trying to look for that."

As we talked, we discussed next class time, especially trying to resolve issues with technology.

Without looking up from typing notes, I had to vent for a minute, "What was up with those stupid breakout rooms! We had it all set up and then, disaster!"

"Don't worry," Karrie said, "It worked out."

"But we were so prepared! We had it all set up! I just hate looking incompetent."

After a few more sessions, we noticed fewer of these issues and began to feel optimistic. Another day, as the last student left, Stefinee said, "OK women, I think it went well."

"Yay!" I laughed with relief, "We got breakout rooms to work this time."

Karrie gave us a thumbs up. "Everyone was super understanding and understood everything." Karrie, who kept us terribly organized, always sounded positive.

I felt I had to give myself an honest critique. "I never seem to learn this. Even though I know better, I guess I assume students know the learning platform and then I tend to rush through the directions. I just forget that I know the timeline and I look at their faces and they look so bored. It never occurs to me that maybe they are confused. But regardless, they need me to share my screen and show them where content is found, where to find articles to download, etc. and not go so fast."

We continued to talk through the next session to make sure everyone knew their jobs.

"It says on my notes we're meeting with Ann next week, I mean, Thursday." For the final project, students designed learning activities for Ann, a practicing teacher. Ann first came to introduce students to the content objectives she had chosen. Groups in the class were to base their activity centers on the objectives she chose. They needed to understand the variability of her students and the context of her school community to do this well. Because Zoom made it easy to have her join us from her home about an hour away, rather than visiting us only twice as we did when the course met in person, we were able to have her visit the class several times.

"That's right. Ann is coming," Stefinee confirmed. "So, what else do we have, Celina?"

"What I want to do is start with a share, post questions in the chat, and that should be fast. They won't have much yet. Then the SEP group will present. Then you're doing the Bible activity to introduce how to plan activity centers so you'll want to have that planned out how you want to do it. Then Ann, then they're going to choose a standard, then groups will breakout."

Stefinee had already thought about how her Bible activity might work online, but we digressed to discuss a few options. "I've got to think about how to do this so it works."

EXPLORING TEACHER EDUCATOR KNOWLEDGE 95

"You might want to make a PowerPoint," I suggested.

"No, the problem is you construct it as you go. Maybe I'll have them draw it as we capture our ideas." Stefinee continued, "You know what happened today during breakouts? You know how we've been worried about Allie? Well today when I joined their breakout room, I wondered aloud why she was missing and suddenly I heard her voice, 'I'm here!' The rest of her group explained she was joining by phone because her connection was so poor. Such a relief! I was really worried about her participation and how her group was doing because we know she's joining us from another time zone."

****

When the course was over, I drove to Stefinee's house to grade final projects and evaluate the changes we had made for the online course. At her kitchen table, I took this opportunity to wonder out loud about teacher educator knowledge and capture our conversation with note taking.

"I actually think I felt less resistance in this online format than I typically do in-person," Stefinee said. Today we shared a sandwich from Jimmy Johns.

"That is surprising, but feels true," I said. "Why is that, I wonder? Students were stuck at home. Maybe that made the difference. For them it was more relaxed – they were able to lean against pillows, wear their slippers, and unobtrusively check a text or leave to use the bathroom. Yet they still produced high quality final assignments. I am relieved and a little surprised."

I typed the question, "In the transition to online, how is my teacher educator knowledge revealed?" and began musing aloud.

"Online or face-to-face, I am still left with the fragility of relationships. The students became good friends in their groups. I think I learned something about not trying to be too fancy with mixing up groups because that consistency of meeting with the same three people actually contributed to their success. I hope I will recognize the students if I see them on campus someday."

Stefinee took notes as I talked. Then she added, "In face-to-face across time where you are teaching the same course, you gain an understanding of where tangles and misunderstanding might emerge – you get better at pacing, you get better at questioning and figuring out where they are. We are always questioning the content – what needs to be reduced, or expanded, when to simplify or be more explicit. I've never taught a class exactly the same even with a course as specified as the TELL courses."

In this spirit of turn-taking, we continued debriefing and note-taking. I added, "Another thing, I think it is hard to teach a project-based course in person or on Zoom and allow so much time to be spent not showing off how much I know. So often in either setting I have to be patient, listen, and prod. I think this transition reveals another shift in technology. I have adapted over the years. As a side note, it was interesting that in this setting the students appeared to appreciate the breakout time we gave them to work together. In person, students often resent being forced to sit at a table in a group, when what they want to do is divvy up tasks and get out of class early."

Stefinee knew what I meant. "Once we could contact students by e-mail this shifted the nature of face-to-face teaching. 'Oh, I forgot to tell the class something! I'll send a reminder in email.' I also think it shifted relationships with students. You could reach out better when they weren't there or you wondered if something hurt them or they misunderstood. Also, we do group work so we have always given space in class to work face-to-face. I had high expectations that they could learn from each other as they interacted and I wasn't sure how that would work online."

We also discussed our theoretical underpinnings. I said, "As we designed the course, it took a lot of effort and time. In the same sense that our time is limited, so we have to make sure that class time is productive."

Stefinee added, "That means everything has to be there and ready for them to use. Sometimes for in-person teaching, I can run back to my office or grab a set of books I want to use out of storage, but all of that has to be prepared and available."

I continued, "At the same time, for example, we intentionally chose to have students prepare on-line presentations, and we knew it could get messy. But we reasoned it was still important. One reason why was that in light of this pandemic, we have an added objective: We want them to have practice teaching and especially practice teaching online because the format is a real possibility. Even for K-12 teachers it is a possibility. These are elementary teachers and perhaps they never envisioned having to do that. We have relinquished control and allowed students to do things. Our class might not be as glossy but not because we did not have the skill."

In response, Stefinee looked at me and reaffirmed, "Theory matters. A commitment to sociocultural teaching is revealed in your choices and actions as a teacher."

Analysis of the Reflecting Vignette

Similar to my analyses of planning and teaching, I analyzed the Reflecting Vignette systematically by highlighting each of the seven strands of teacher educator knowledge. In this analysis, I showed how they interrelate and how the connections shift somewhat since reflecting occurs in the midst of examining what happened in the teaching and making adjustments for planning future sessions or future courses. In order to draw attention to how the strands emerge and interact, I indicated them in italicized font. At the end, I summarized the understandings that emerged from examining my teacher educator knowledge while reflecting on the course. Again, these strands of teacher educator knowledge are *Content Knowledge, Fixed and Fluid Elements, Knowledge of Milieu, Pedagogical Intent, Preservice Teacher Knowledge and Belief, Value and Fragility of Relationships,* and *Theory Matters.*

In the vignette, it became immediately apparent in the moments just following teaching how physically exhausting it was to teach in an online synchronous classroom for several hours. As the last student waved goodbye and left the Zoom meeting, I described a "let-down of teacher tension," and reported, "I always feel wrung out after the first session." Part of the exhaustion expressed here was related to the effort it took to watch students' faces and body language for signs of understanding, engagement, or not (*Milieu; Preservice Teacher Knowledge and Belief*). Stefinee explained, "In Zoom we can't see clearly enough their facial features, the nuances of their body language." Unlike asynchronous online classes, we still had chosen to meet for the scheduled class hours in order to provide interaction and allow groups to work together and demonstrate their learning in real time (*Theory; Pedagogical Intent*). However, only meeting students online added to a feeling of disconnect that we often worried about during debriefing. Stefinee compared this intent, emotional work of connecting in higher education, to the experience of a practicing teacher working closely with a student to determine "what a child knows" (*Milieu; Content Knowledge; Value and Fragility of Relationships*).

Just after teaching, it was typical for the three of us, two co-teachers and one TA, to report to each other on what went well and vent about what was frustrating (*Fixed and Fluid Elements*). This was represented in the first part of the vignette. For me, it took about two sessions to be able to get a handle on the elements of Zoom that were unfamiliar (*Milieu; Content*). At one point, I had to vent, "What was up with those stupid breakout rooms! We had it all set up and then, disaster!" The vignette revealed my frustration when technology I had prepared did not work how I expected and my worry that if I appeared technologically incompetent, students would take that as an indicator of my credibility as a teacher educator (*Pedagogical Intent; Value and Fragility of Relationships*).

The wrestling with technology warranted a little venting, but my experience as a teacher and what I know about teaching higher education in particular also revealed my ability to relax and wait (*Content Knowledge*). Because of our past experiences with transitions in using technology to support teaching, such as Stefinee appreciating the affordances provided by email, I was able to be patient and willing to explore new possibilities as well as limitations of online learning (*Value and Fragility of Relationships*). I knew I was capable of learning how to teach more effectively via Zoom, and indeed, later I reported that I "noticed fewer of these issues and began to feel more optimistic." In the vignette, my willingness to learn new ways of teaching and use online tools was evidence of deepening teacher educator knowledge in a new setting (*Milieu*).

During reflecting, I also noticed some changes for the preservice teachers participating in the online course (*Preservice Teacher Knowledge and Belief; Milieu*). I observed that students seemed to enjoy participation in their small groups and engage more willingly in breakout rooms than I remembered them doing in an in-person setting. I noted the contrast, "In person, students often resent being forced to sit at a table in a group, when what they want to do is divvy up tasks and get out of class early." (*Preservice Teacher Knowledge and Belief; Content Knowledge; Value and Fragility of Relationships*). Some of the time, debriefing was a matter of "making sure everyone knew their jobs," but in this case, the discussion during reflecting helped uncover ways the online course was both difficult and supportive of student learning (*Value and Fragility of Relationships; Pedagogical Intent*).

In the vignette, I critiqued my decision to rush through the directions and learning platform and considered myself to fall short. Even though *Fixed Elements* were in place, the directions and the platform, I did not handle as well the *Fluid Elements*. Since I am not perfect in my knowledge, this exemplar was significant because the students' confusion was not immediately apparent to me and I ended up repeating a mistake that I had made before when I rushed and over-worried about time or bored students (*Milieu, Content; Preservice Teacher Knowledge and Belief*). Even though I "knew" from past experience that it was important to take some valuable class time to walk students through the learning platform and go over the directions to the assignments, I chose not to, went too fast, and had to stop and help confused students. I needed to spend valuable time that supported and potentially repaired *Relationships*. In reflecting, I said, "I never seem to learn this ... I guess I assume students know ... and I look at their faces and they look so bored." In the act of teaching, I did not always act on knowledge that I already understood about familiarizing students with the assignments and the learning platform, until student confusion or frustration recalled this knowledge to me (*Content Knowledge; Milieu; Value of Relationships; Preservice Teacher Knowledge and Belief*).

In the vignette, I was able to recognize that as a teacher educator it was important to take the time to walk through whatever questions students have because this is my opportunity to clarify Content. The vignette captured an instance when I did not recognize this and act on it while teaching. Only in debriefing did I recognize and remember the importance of taking the time to consider student learning of *Content*. I recognized as well the need to share my screen and show students where they could access homework, articles, and other resources on the learning platform (*Preservice Teacher Knowledge and Belief*). While not discussed in the vignette, this kind of evaluation could inform a future iteration of the class, and I could eliminate some stress, rush, and confusion by building an explanation of the course resources and assignments into the course design as a *Fixed Element*.

In the vignette, it was revealed that our debriefing and discussion between sessions often focused on our concerns about *Relationships* with students in this new *Milieu*. Stefinee related how one student that we had been concerned about was actually fully participating with her group, even though we could see that she often dropped out of the Zoom meetings. Stefinee said, "You know how we've been worried about Allie? Such a relief! I was really worried about her participation and how her group was doing." For the most part, all students were able to participate with both video and audio for the majority of each session. This experience was another good reminder that the fast internet connection I enjoyed in my community was not the same as Allie's spotty connection, and online capacity may vary widely for class participants (*Preservice Teacher Knowledge and Belief*).

Circling back around to theoretical underpinnings, I recognized while reflecting that some of the uncertainty of the course design could have been eliminated if we had relied more on direct instruction (*Knowledge of Theory; Pedagogical Intent*). By choosing a project-based design and providing time for

EXPLORING TEACHER EDUCATOR KNOWLEDGE 99

students to collaborate together, I already knew it could "get messy." However, in planning, we had decided that this shift to an online course would not affect the main purposes of the course and its foundations in sociocultural theory. In teaching, we had already committed to supporting students in collaborating together on their projects and provided them with the resources, time, interaction, and teaching required to be successful. Upon reflection, I said, "Our class might not be as glossy but not because we did not have the skill." Indeed, by adding more *Fixed Elements*, we could have removed some uncertainty and messiness. Stefinee's response reaffirmed what we had set out to do at the start, "Theory matters. A commitment to sociocultural teaching is revealed in your choices and actions as a teacher."

Summary of Teacher Educator Knowledge in Reflecting

In summary, during those experiences when we reflected on the online course, the seven strands of teacher educator knowledge were represented: *Content Knowledge, Fixed and Flexible Elements, Knowledge of Milieu, Pedagogical Intent, Preservice Teacher Knowledge and Belief, Value and Fragility of Relationships*, and *Theory Matters*. The strands were revealed throughout analysis of the field data, while composing the vignette, and in unpacking the vignette. While all seven strands of teacher educator knowledge were present while reflecting about the course, some strands were more evident than others. I will consider each strand and how it emerged during reflection.

(1) *Knowledge of Content.* The expertise a teacher educator holds on subject matter, engaging preservice teachers with the subject matter, as well as personal practical knowledge gained from past experience is conceptualized as knowledge of content. While evaluating teaching that occurred or the intended outcomes of a course design, this knowledge emerged. The strand was not as visible since many decisions about what content to include were made and had been tested in previous iterations of teaching the course. Rather, the strand was understood to be present in the vignette as we evaluated how technology was working, how student relationships were thriving, and how projects and activities were functioning. I drew forward subject matter knowledge and attended to how students' new knowledge was being shaped. During experiences of debriefing or reflecting, we noticed that we were tracking content knowledge in terms of how the activities were helping students meet our pedagogical intents, how the knowledge and beliefs of preservice teachers were shifting in the ways we wanted them to, and whether the fixed and fluid elements operated in support of their learning.

(2) *Knowledge of Fixed and Fluid Elements.* This strand refers to the areas of course design that can be planned and set in place and those elements that are allowed to vary so that the teacher educator can be responsive in the moment to student learning. Decisions about fixed and fluid elements were made in planning, in the moments of teaching, and continued to be attended to in reflecting. Indeed, reflecting on the course became an important step in

uncovering teacher educator knowledge because I was involved in discussions about how the course was working and whether or not students were learning the key ideas I wanted them to learn. In these discussions represented in the vignette, I pointed to glitches in student's ability to access materials and whether sufficient materials were available. Reflecting and debriefing were important moments for looking forward to the next iteration of this course, especially in terms of affordances and constraints of fixed and fluid elements. I recognized that not everything could be anticipated. In the vignette, changes were made to the fixed elements of the course between sessions such asking the practicing teacher to join by Zoom and offer feedback to the students' curriculum projects one additional time. This strand naturally entwined with milieu and pedagogical intent.

(3) *Knowledge of Milieu.* Attention to milieu is evident in my awareness of the cultural context and environment of learners as they interact with the teacher and the content (Schwab, 1973). In the Reflecting Vignette, this strand was evident in my concern about how to improve technology use, communication, and assignments and make appropriate adjustments for teaching online. In particular, I was aware of milieu when adjusting assignments and evaluating group work. Thus, milieu was closely related to decisions related to content, theory, preservice teacher knowledge and beliefs, fixed and fluid elements, and the value of relationships.

(4) *Knowledge of Pedagogical Intent.* I realized during reflecting that attention to pedagogical intent, whether or not activities were meeting their learning purposes, allowed me to simultaneously attend to content, fixed and fluid elements, milieu, preservice teacher knowledge and belief, and theory. This is because discussion of whether students met the pedagogical intent for a given activity involved the alignment of the other strands. Attention to pedagogical intent in reflecting enabled me as a teacher educator to appraise and evaluate the success of individual activities and how they were working collectively in promoting student learning. This strand was evident when I questioned how assignments and groups were functioning and if desired outcomes were being met. Indeed, it was during reflection that I recognized an additional reason for having students prepare and deliver presentations was because of the real possibility that even elementary teachers may have to do that. Thus, the knowledge about the pedagogical intent of activities in the course was a strand that emerged explicitly during planning, observed and adjusted during teaching, and served as a tool for evaluation after sessions and after the course was complete. This strand related to all the other strands.

(5) *Knowledge of Preservice Teacher Knowledge and Belief.* This refers to my understanding that my preservice teacher students already have personal experiences, practical knowledge, and textbook knowledge about teaching. In reflecting within my role as a teacher educator, I attended to whether the teacher education practices I was engaged in that were particularly attuned to supporting integration, change and growth in preservice teacher knowledge and belief as they were becoming teachers. I was very aware of this as I was preparing for the course and while teaching the course. But in analyzing my

EXPLORING TEACHER EDUCATOR KNOWLEDGE

reflections on the course, I realized I was especially attuned to this strand because I was constantly evaluating preservice teachers' progress in acquiring the knowledge and belief about teaching English learners that would be most helpful in their teaching. In reflecting, this strand was evident as I made decisions of how to support the preservice teachers now that students were engaged with me, the content, and the course assignments within a real-time milieu. Thus, this strand was often entwined with knowledge of relationships, milieu, theory, and content.

(6) *Knowledge of Theory.* This strand refers to my understanding of theories of learning based in interaction and language as they inform my decisions in course design to engage preservice teachers in sociocultural pedagogical practices, model them, thus laying the groundwork for them to employ sociocultural learning practices with the students they will teach. My knowledge of theory was often implicit in reflecting such as when we considered some of the changes we noticed in the shift from in-person teaching to online. Looking back on the course allowed me to explicitly consider theory and recognize intentional choices of content and design that were based in a commitment to sociocultural teaching. The strand of theory is strongly connected with the other strands of teacher educator knowledge and is often implicit such as in discussions that seem to be focused on pedagogical intent, relationships, or preservice teacher knowledge.

(7) *Value and Fragility of Relationships.* This strand is ever-present. As a teacher educator, I recognized the fundamental need to have relationships with preservice teachers and the fragility of these relationships as they deal with their life demands and requirements of the program. I was constantly aware of the importance of building connections between teachers and students and students with other students to create an optimal learning environment for meeting the goals of the course. This strand of knowledge emerged often while debriefing, revealing my attention to relationships in the course and also evidence of the importance of relationships between co-teachers. Debriefing after class had a dual purpose, therefore, of revealing the value of relationships among us as co-teachers and as an important step in completing the process of identifying pedagogical intent. By evaluating and reflecting between classes, I identified what kinds of course adjustments needed to happen, what technology issues needed improvement, and considered other issues that affected the relationships between students. It also became evident to me during debriefing sessions that I valued the relationships that were strengthened while co-teaching, as evidenced by Stefinee's encouraging words, a trusting environment where it was safe to share where I felt my teaching was falling short, and an ongoing commitment to be positive with each other during a global pandemic, a time of heightened tension and demanding circumstances. The strand of knowledge of relationships is closely connected to theory but was also evident in evaluations of pedagogy, content, fixed and fluid elements, technology, and preservice teacher knowledge and belief.

WHAT ARE THE STRANDS OF TEACHER EDUCATOR KNOWLEDGE EMBEDDED ACROSS THE VIGNETTES?

ABSTRACT

This chapter presents an explicit description of each strand of teacher educator knowledge and considers how the context represented in an analytic narrative vignette provided constraints and affordances in terms of my ability as a self-study of teacher education practice to reveal what I came to understand about teacher educator knowledge. I explored individually the seven strands of teacher educator knowledge, which are Content Knowledge, Fixed and Flexible Elements, Knowledge of Milieu, Pedagogical Intent, Preservice Teacher Knowledge and Belief, Value and Fragility of Relationships, *and* Theory. *The discussion is guided by the holistic initial research question, "What does my transition to online teaching reveal about my teacher educator knowledge?" To communicate these strands of teacher educator knowledge in my transition to teaching online, I first defined the strand generally, showed how it operates in terms of planning, teaching and reflecting, and ended with an explanation of how this knowledge informed my identity and commitments as a teacher educator. As a narrative self-study of practice focused on the goals of personal improvement as well as to inform the larger research community, in this discussion, I focus on the learning that emerged during the shifts to teaching online. I have avoided as much as possible making claims about what I uncovered as representing the entirety of teacher educator knowledge.*

Keywords: Teacher educator knowledge; preservice teacher knowledge; pedagogical content knowledge; teacher knowledge; theory; self-study of practice; narrative research; online teacher education; course design; analytic narrative vignettes

In the previous chapters, the strands of teacher educator knowledge were represented in analytic narrative vignettes that captured the context of planning,

---

Exploring Teacher Educator Knowledge
Advances in Research on Teaching, Volume 48, 103–112
Copyright © 2025 Celina Dulude Lay
Published under exclusive licence by Emerald Publishing Limited
ISSN: 1479-3687/doi:10.1108/S1479-368720240000048008

teaching, and reflecting on my experiences moving a course previously taught in-person to an online format. After the vignettes were presented, they were unpacked to reveal the teacher educator knowledge strands embedded in them and reflective of the raw data of the study. Through this analytic process, I have identified seven strands of teacher educator knowledge that emerged.

For the previous three chapters, I considered how the strands emerged and interacted within each context. In this discussion, I have turned to a more explicit description of each strand and considered how the context represented by an analytic narrative vignette provided constraints and affordances in terms of my ability as a self-study of teacher education practice to reveal what I came to understand about teacher educator knowledge. Since this is a narrative self-study of practice focused on the goals of personal improvement as well as to inform the larger research community, in this discussion, I responded more holistically to the initial research question, "What does my transition to online teaching reveal about my teacher educator knowledge?" while describing each of the seven strands of teacher educator knowledge.

This discussion revolves around an assertion made by Connelly et al. (1997) that "teacher knowledge and knowing affects every aspect of the teaching act" (p. 666). This assertion seemed to hold true for my experience here as a teacher educator shifting to teaching a course online as well. Since I was looking at shifts, both in-person and online teaching characteristics of teacher educator knowledge emerged. However, since my focus in this study was on the transition to online instruction, I have avoided as much as possible making claims about what I uncovered as representing the entirety of teacher educator knowledge generally. As I explored each analytic narrative vignette, what became clear was the way the strands of teacher educator knowledge were entangled, connected, and integrated with each other. This was readily apparent in my analysis of each vignette. In this chapter, I discuss each of the strands of teacher educator knowledge that emerged in this study separately as a way to represent my findings more holistically.

TEACHER EDUCATOR KNOWLEDGE

As a reminder, Vanassche and Berry's (2020) description of teacher educator knowledge as "tacit, complex, often contradictory, situated, relational, and moral" (p. 181) was an important foundational description for understanding my own knowledge as a teacher educator. It reminded me that teacher educator knowledge was fundamentally concerned with the moral and the ethical and is represented here by statements concerning teacher educator responsibilities, obligations, and commitments. As I turned to each of the seven strands of teacher educator knowledge, I recognized how my definitions, exemplars, and perspectives are thoroughly situated in my own complex, moral, and social context.

In addition, Berry's (2007) explication of the tensions that teacher educators negotiate in their teaching informed my thinking and analysis. As I explored and analyzed these strands, my own identity and commitments as a teacher educator became evident in the shift to teaching online but were important to me for both

EXPLORING TEACHER EDUCATOR KNOWLEDGE

contexts, in person and online. Because I was exploring the ways my engagement in online instruction revealed my teacher educator knowledge and the shifts in that knowledge, I realized that much of the information in the seven strands would be similar whether teaching in-person or online. However, I realized the context of the online setting made me hyperaware of features within each strand. For example, my intensified focus on the value and fragility of relationships and how they were explicitly attended to in new ways, such as my use of the three-person groups and extended project-based work, it was also present in my considerations about theory and in my critical attention to pedagogical intent. I also realized that this careful consideration and analysis of my teacher educator knowledge was an aid to strengthening my teacher educator identity and deepening my commitments.

As I analyzed the vignettes, the strands all became evident, some more apparently than others. I noted episodes of relationship building, preservice teacher beliefs, my engagement with students and with the content, and my core attention to theory, especially my understanding about sociocultural learning, learning online and using technology, and the interplay of the commonplaces of teacher, student, milieu, and curriculum in action. Uncovering my teacher educator knowledge made me more aware of my purposes and pedagogical intent behind instructional decisions I was making. It provided me with new understandings and strategies for analyzing my actions and interactions with students and curriculum. My descriptions of teacher educator knowledge are probably not comprehensive and were never intended to present a "best" way to teach an online course; but rather, this process helped me learn from my decisions in the actions of planning, teaching, and reflecting, uncover what I really understand and know about preparing preservice teachers, and clearly revealed my commitments and obligations as a teacher educator.

In this chapter, I explored individually the seven strands of teacher educator knowledge, which are *Content Knowledge, Fixed and Flexible Elements, Knowledge of Milieu, Pedagogical Intent, Preservice Teacher Knowledge and Belief, Value and Fragility of Relationships*, and *Theory*. Because I considered them separately, unlike in the previous chapter as an aid to analysis, I did not use an italicized font for the titles of the strands of teacher educator knowledge. To communicate these strands of teacher educator knowledge in my transition to teaching online, I have first defined the strand generally, showed how it operates in terms of planning, teaching and reflecting, and ended with an explanation of how this knowledge informed my identity and commitments as a teacher educator.

Content Knowledge

The expertise a teacher educator has acquired on subject matter is an important beginning for exploring a teacher educator's knowledge. Much like the various explanations of teacher knowledge founded on Shulman's (1986) articulation of its components, teacher educator knowledge of content, learning, and teaching are fundamental yet not all of what it is comprises. A teacher educator also has subject matter knowledge that includes an understanding of potential challenges or difficulties as well as ease. This means teacher educators have knowledge of subject matter, what is essential for preservice teachers to know and where the potential points of struggle may arise. Some of this knowledge was developed in their undergraduate preparation, in their further study of the content, as well as personal practical knowledge gained from past experiences teaching or in other fields.

During planning, my content knowledge was not often explicitly articulated, likely because the content of this course had already been made in previous iterations of the course. However, as I analyzed the data, it became evident to me that I was making curriculum decisions based on my knowledge of the content, even if it was not explicit. Therefore, my prior experiences teaching the course and knowledge of evidence-based practices for supporting adult learners and preservice teachers informed my decisions about course design. During teaching, my understanding of the content of the course enabled me to gauge how students were learning and experiencing the activities and the content in the class. In these interactions with students, I was reminded that teacher educators require a deep knowledge of the subject matter in order to be ready, in the moment, to move preservice teachers forward in their own learning (Shulman, 1986). During experiences of reflecting, it was evident that a teacher educator's knowledge of pedagogical applications of technology was important for supporting students in their learning.

This strand made clear to me my own obligations as a teacher educator toward the preservice teachers I taught. In the dialogue with my critical friend that was fundamental to my analysis and through the construction and analysis of the narrative vignettes, I articulated my own commitment to be a teacher educator who knows the subject matter well, not for myself in a competitive sense of knowing the most, but so that I can better assist preservice teachers as they move forward in their own learning. As with Schwab's (1973) commonplaces of teacher, student, milieu, and content, the analysis revealed that I seek the ability to make purposeful pedagogical decisions in planning, teaching, and reflecting, particularly in the moment so that it can guide me in tailoring curriculum for a particular student in a particular context. Examination of this strand highlighted for me the value of content knowledge and a recognition of the deep knowledge of content, pedagogy, and teaching that teacher educators have to offer.

Fixed and Fluid Elements

Knowledge of fixed and fluid elements is an important strand of knowledge for teacher educators. It refers to the details, requirements, and documents of course design that are set in place when a course is designed and must be available. When careful and appropriate identification of the necessary fixed elements is made, that then frees up space so that in the moment teacher educators can adjust during the teaching of the course. While present in all course design, including in-person and online classes, decisions about fixed and fluid elements are fundamentally important in online contexts, because it is only if those are in place

EXPLORING TEACHER EDUCATOR KNOWLEDGE

that the teacher educator has the luxury of flexibility. This strand is informed by a teacher educator's theoretical stance and understanding about how preservice teachers move forward in their learning and what they will need in terms of content, activities, study, support, and interaction.

During planning, I attended very explicitly to the content, materials needed, activities, schedule and other decisions that could be made in advance. Especially given the upheaval of teaching during a global pandemic, I knew how vital it was to make the content of the course accessible to students both by being clear with directions and making resources easily available. During teaching, there was evidence that the fixed and fluid elements aided the instructor's ability to forestall confusion, allow for flexibility to make quick adjustments to activities, or be responsive in moments of instruction. However, my examination and analysis highlighted how imperative it is to have in place the fixed elements in order to make space for fluid responses. Significantly for teacher educators, for online course design and teaching, both fixed and fluid elements must be carefully attended to before the course begins, even more than when teaching in person. During reflecting, decisions about fixed and fluid elements were examined as glitches arose and were resolved, and determination about potential additional fixed elements were made. During reflection, I examined fixed and fluid elements as I looked ahead to future iterations of the course, especially in terms of the affordances and constraints that were uncovered while teaching.

This strand of teacher educator knowledge was an important area for me to consider. I learned that not everything could be anticipated. As a teacher educator, I already knew this, but by naming this knowledge and recognizing the choices I had made about what to fix and what to allow to vary in terms of course design, I was able to make pedagogical decisions in the moment and spend more of the time spent in class supporting students and offering feedback rather than dealing with issues of insufficient resources or an unclear schedule. I recognized that the knowledge of how to wisely attend to fixed and fluid elements helps teacher educators honor their obligations to preservice teachers and the students their preservice teachers will someday teach.

Knowledge of Milieu

Knowledge of milieu is based on Schwab's (1973) conception of how teachers and learners interact with the content in a given milieu. For teacher educators, their milieu is often the context of an institution of higher education as well as public school classrooms they are preparing their preservice teachers for. These dual contexts of a teacher educator's milieu add additional layering of context. This is relevant as teacher educators make decisions within that milieu since it offers both affordances and constraints. In particular, I was aware of creating activities such as creating real curriculum for a practicing teacher and using resources that I felt supported preservice teachers in gaining insights into the milieu of classroom teaching. However, an additional reality of this milieu was that at my institution, this course now had to be taught in an online format and preservice teachers would not be able to interact in public school classrooms.

During planning, this shift in teaching context caused me to consider even more carefully how to support students in creating their curriculum projects and in giving them experience and practice using online tools themselves. During teaching, students joined class via Zoom and all of us, preservice teachers and instructors, were experiencing unusual challenges because of the global pandemic. This jarring shift in milieu forced me to consider even more carefully how students were doing and monitor frequently their understanding and ability to access materials or connect with classmates. As I reflected between each session and after the course was complete, I gained insights about how to improve technology use, communication, and assignments and make appropriate adjustments for teaching online. My knowledge of milieu helped me adjust assignments and evaluate group work.

Even though I could usually see students' faces on-screen while teaching, the online context at times made me feel even more separated from students. Because of this added effort to read moods and faces and gauge understanding, I recognized that this high level of presence is difficult to sustain, and this led me to wonder about other ways to improve the online milieu for both students and teachers. One other relevant realization I had as I examined this strand of my teacher educator knowledge was that preservice teachers now need learning experiences in remote learning, including how to organize a class, communicate online, and present and teach content. In my past understanding of preparing preservice teachers, I never would have conceived that preservice teachers, even elementary education majors, would need preparation for potentially teaching a class from a distance. In the shift to teaching online during a global pandemic, I gained understanding about the significance of milieu for teacher educators, preservice teachers, and for the students they would 1 day teach.

Pedagogical Intent

Pedagogical intent was conceptualized by Allman and Pinnegar (2020) as the efforts of a course designer to identify the intended learning experience desired and align the content delivery and the learning activity accordingly. When a designer carefully considers the goals of a learning task, then decisions about required content and a choice of pedagogical or digital tools can be more strategically selected. One of the understandings that was uncovered was that when pedagogical intent emerged in my analysis, it was accompanied with concerns regarding content, fixed and fluid elements, milieu, preservice teacher belief and knowledge, value and fragility of relationships, and theory: all of the strands of teacher educator knowledge.

During planning, my attention to pedagogical intent led me to make critical decisions before class even started such as reducing the number of assignments, determining how students would collaborate, and the prioritizing of content. Knowledge of this strand then can assist teacher educators in moving forward the thinking and learning of preservice teachers by careful articulation of the pedagogical intent of each learning experience and the consideration of what needs to be present for the experience to meet the intent. During teaching, I considered

EXPLORING TEACHER EDUCATOR KNOWLEDGE

pedagogical intent as I monitored how activities were working, how well students were engaging, and if the goals were being met. I began to understand pedagogical intent as a way to attend to the particular and the global simultaneously. It provided a tool to evaluate the purposes of the course being enacted by students in the context of a specific learning task in a particular session with particular content. Attention to pedagogical intent in reflecting allowed me as a teacher educator to consider the success of individual activities and how they were working collectively in supporting student learning and pointed toward actions I could take to repair or better meet the learning goals of the course.

A teacher educator's knowledge of pedagogical intent is a distinct asset for designing coursework, gathering content that is relevant and supportive of preservice teacher learning, and managing the tensions between all the decisions being made in the moments of teaching. I recognized during analysis of this strand that I have an ongoing commitment to improving my own teaching practice. A deep understanding of pedagogical intent supports teacher educators as they bring together content, fixed and fluid elements, milieu, preservice teacher knowledge and belief, relationships, and theory. Pedagogical intent is the kind of knowledge that enables teacher educators to make fine-tuned decisions about activities and course design that are otherwise difficult to pinpoint or adjust.

Preservice Teacher Knowledge and Belief

Teacher educator knowledge of preservice teacher knowledge and belief likely varies widely given the range of experience and education of teacher educators. For me, my knowledge of preservice teacher knowledge and belief stems from a recognition that preservice teachers have personal experiences that brought them to choose teaching as a profession and that they already know a lot about teaching. It also stems from the fact that I was a practicing teacher so that I recognize often how my preservice teachers are positioning themselves, the beliefs they hold, and the knowledge strengths and deficits they potentially bring to teacher preparation. In my role as a teacher educator, I want to welcome their personal experiences, practical knowledge, and textbook knowledge about teaching and engage them in practices that are particularly attuned to supporting integration, change, and growth in preservice teacher knowledge and belief as they become teachers (Clandinin, 2000).

During planning, I chose activities and content based on my understanding of the knowledge and belief that preservice teachers would bring to the course. In the context of this course, I made decisions about the course design and resources to be made available while remembering what preservice teachers had already learned about English learners, literacy, and what myths or assumptions they were likely to still hold regarding second language acquisition or the English learners they would someday teach. During teaching, I interacted directly with students, listening to their insights, connections, confusions, and perspectives in order to help shape and reshape the knowledge they already had. During reflecting, I often found myself evaluating preservice teachers' progress in acquiring the knowledge and belief about teaching English learners that would be most helpful in their teaching. I noticed that by having fixed and fluid elements of the course prepared in advance, I was able to engage with students in productive ways and find helpful resources quickly to aid and support their development of activity centers and deepen their knowledge of teaching English learners.

As I learned more about my own knowledge of this strand, I recognized my commitment to respecting preservice teacher perspectives, ideas, questions, and growth. It is significant that before I even met the preservice teachers I would be teaching, I was able to make informed decisions about course design based in my past experience preparing preservice teachers and based on a stated commitment to support and engage preservice teachers in whatever way they are ready to learn. I believe my comfort with this stance has grown as I also have grown in my knowledge as a teacher educator. More and more, I see that knowledge of how to gauge and support preservice teachers wherever they are in their thinking and learning can improve teacher educators' ability to draw forward preservice teachers' prior knowledge, integrate and expand it in preparing them to teach.

Value and Fragility of Relationships

Most teacher educators understand that relationships are fundamental to strong teacher education (Kitchen, 2005). Therefore, it was not surprising to me that this emerged as a strand of teacher educator knowledge. However, the new understanding that was uncovered in this study were the descriptors of value and fragility. As I worked on this course in all phases of planning, teaching, and reflecting, a fundamental concern was always targeted at the relationships, how they were shaping up, how they were threatened, how they could be bolstered. I have always been aware that relationships were important but in shifting to teaching online, I recognized the vital importance of this strand of knowledge. This strand of knowledge emerges from my understanding of the value of building connections between students with the teacher and also students with each other in order to create an optimal learning environment. The fragility of relationships refers to a recognition that no matter how much preparation or experience a teacher educator may have, a thriving classroom community is dependent on many factors out of the teacher educator's control. In the context of this course, a course design based in sociocultural theory was expressly chosen as an evidence-based pedagogy for supporting preservice teacher learning and also for supporting English learners in developing literacy and language.

During planning, even though I had not yet met the students, I was thinking ahead about how to help relationships flourish even in a quick 5-week online course. I made the decision at the beginning to have students spend at least an hour of our time together working in small three-person breakout room groups. Preservice teachers later voluntarily commented on how important that was to their learning. It had value for teaching because students could support each other, and their strong relationships could potentially carry them across difficulties they might have in learning. During teaching, I invited questions and openness in order to support learning and try to create a tone in the class that welcomed participation. This work during teaching is all-consuming as a teacher

EXPLORING TEACHER EDUCATOR KNOWLEDGE

educator makes quick adjustments in the moment and constant decisions about when to listen, when to intrude, when to redirect, or when to push thinking. During reflecting, I constantly referred to relationships and my own role as the teacher educator and the roles of students, trying to meet my obligations to them and direct them to meet their obligations to each other and to the goals of the course.

A commitment to supporting relationships and attending to their value and fragility was evident through all my decisions in the course. Choices about my presence or absence of interaction with students revealed that this was uncertain work. According to Vanassche and Berry (2020), the theoretical knowledge a teacher educator holds is "brought to life through ... actions in practice" (p. 189). From the beginning, I articulated a commitment to communicating expectations, inviting trust, giving ample time for groups to work together, and designing the course activities around much repeated and multiple opportunities to collaborate, discuss, and interact. I recognized that in holding this commitment to relationships, I also must invite the uncertainty and fragility of whether or not these connections will be taken up and thrive along with it. Also, in this uncertainty, I recognize a commitment to enacting and modeling sociocultural relational pedagogy as much as I am able – even knowing I am not perfect at it and that it invites uncertainty – because otherwise students will never really know how these pedagogies can be taken up in a classroom.

Especially given this context of an online environment, student questions were one of the most important windows into student thinking and also for establishing and supporting teacher–student relationships. As a teacher educator, I do not want to fall into the trap of telling students best ways to do things and not at least try to enact those ways myself. This is a vulnerability inherent in this strand of knowledge. Teacher educator choices involved in teaching may have many purposes but are often fundamentally about navigating the value and fragility of the relationships that need to be present for preservice teachers to learn.

Theory Matters

Teacher educator knowledge of theory refers to understandings about the nature of knowledge and how learning occurs. In particular, both this course and my own actions as a teacher educator are informed by a sociocultural approach to learning and an understanding of how preservice teachers and adults learn and shift in their thinking. The course design and my own actions also reflected the importance of engaging preservice teachers in theory-based practices for English learners.

During planning, theory was fundamental in making decisions related to pedagogy, technology, content, and student engagement. From the project-based course design to the reduced size of groups in breakout rooms, these decisions were all about how to set up an online classroom in order to model for students those pedagogies best for helping English learners engage in reading, writing, listening, and speaking using academic language and for preservice teachers to have ample opportunity to talk about their own thinking and interact frequently with the content and activities in the course. During teaching, we explained to students how the course was designed along principles of sociocultural theory, both as a way to model these pedagogies and to make explicit our own commitment to learning as a social act. During reflecting, a deep understanding of the theory driving my practice was useful as I looked back to consider how choices of content and design may have met the goals of the class or may be improved.

Before teaching the course, I initially did not identify theory as a strand of teacher educator knowledge. However, when I reviewed the first data I collected, almost the first sentences were about commitments to theory. I recognized that while I have long taught these courses that have been designed according to sociocultural theoretical principles, my own teacher educator knowledge of theory was deepened as I attended to pedagogical intent of activities and especially during the challenge of shifting to teaching online in the context of a global pandemic. While I had already had experience moving one of the TELL courses into an online format, this experience led me to really consider the constraints and affordances of creating communities of practice in online settings. Even though it may be easier to just deliver content, teacher educators should be able to identify the theories behind their assumptions about teaching and learning and their own content. Teacher educators cannot separate their commitment and understanding of how important particular pedagogical practices are for moving preservice teacher knowledge forward and for helping these beginners gain knowledge of theoretically based teaching and learning.

WHAT DOES THIS STUDY CONTRIBUTE TO OUR UNDERSTANDING ABOUT TEACHER EDUCATION?

ABSTRACT

When this self-study was undertaken, research of the exploration of teacher educator knowledge was in its infancy. Teacher knowledge, such as content area expertise or experience in a K-12 classroom, is an important contributor to a teacher educator's knowledge. However, the particular knowledge held as a teacher educator is positioned differently. The strands of teacher educator knowledge revealed in this study reveal the complicated, variable ways teacher educators design curriculum and interactions that will move forward the knowledge and learning of preservice teachers. Central to the context of this study was the move from teaching a course I had taught before in-person to an online platform. It is a relevant contribution to establish that the strands were revealed in the shift, that the strands were made clear and personal beliefs validated as I made those decisions about preservice teacher curriculum in a new teaching format. Such tacit knowledge is potentially better examined in such settings. This study, in particular its approach as a self-study of practice, also contributes by examining the strands of teacher educator knowledge as a way to uncover knowledge, sources of motivation for teacher educators, and a commitment to improving practice. By positioning the study in the particular context of a shift to teaching online, the strands uncovered in this study can inform the larger research conversation and lead to further explorations of the knowledge, obligations, and responsibilities held by teacher educators in similar or different settings.

Keywords: Self-study of practice; teacher educator knowledge; teacher knowledge; teacher education; curriculum design; tacit knowledge; moral dimensions of teaching; online education; exemplars; narrative research

At the time of this study, there was a recognition within the S-STEP community that teacher knowledge and teacher educator knowledge were not the same thing

---

Exploring Teacher Educator Knowledge
Advances in Research on Teaching, Volume 48, 113–121
Copyright © 2025 Celina Dulude Lay
Published under exclusive licence by Emerald Publishing Limited
ISSN: 1479-3687/doi:10.1108/S1479-368720240000048009

(Loughran, 2013; Loughran et al., 2012; Vanassche & Berry, 2020). At the time of my self-study, the case for the existence of teacher educator knowledge had already been made (Berry, 2007), as had the argument for a pedagogy of teacher education (Loughran, 2013). Indeed, the exploration of teacher educator knowledge was still in its infancy. The purpose of this chapter is to contextualize a study of teacher educator knowledge and contribute a more sophisticated understanding of some of the strands of teacher educator knowledge. In order to do this, I revisit the need to develop an understanding of teacher educator knowledge. Next, I argue for positioning this self-study in the context of a shift in curriculum-making in teacher education. Then, I revisit some of the significant findings on teacher educator knowledge revealed in this study.

A NEED TO DEVELOP AN UNDERSTANDING OF TEACHER EDUCATOR KNOWLEDGE

As discussed in Chapter 2, the tensions at the heart of teacher education are intrinsic sites of potential growth for teacher educators. In that chapter, an overview of teacher education was presented that indicated three areas of ongoing tension. First, teacher education holds a historically problematic position within institutions of higher education that has direct impact on the lack of influence of teacher educators coupled with hyper pressure to perform both as scholar and as teachers. A part of that pressure is that there are many and varied alternative routes for people to become a teacher, and yet teacher education is held accountable for them all.

Second, the tension between teacher preparation as training or education is an ongoing debate. Teacher education positioned as training usually results in programs divided into compartmentalized pieces of knowledge that somehow preservice teachers are supposed to integrate and act on. At the other end of the spectrum, in programs organized from an education orientation, teacher educators strive to begin with the beliefs preservice teachers hold, then build on this knowledge from their prior schooling and their personal experiences acting as teachers (Clandinin, 2000).

Third, the tension between university coursework and public school field experiences requires constant negotiation as teacher educators must determine which focus is more important and how much of each should be part of a quality program. One of the ongoing challenges in teacher education is what is identified as the theory practice divide. Thomas (2017), in examining her own practices as the director of field experiences within her teacher education program, came to recognize that the way in which she designed field experiences actually continually reinstated that divide, supporting a system in direct opposition to her commitments.

The complexity of what is needed to understand teacher educator knowledge is made clearer in the strands revealed in this study. For example, teachers must take into account the *Knowledge and Belief of Preservice Teachers* within a content area in order to create curriculum that will move preservice teachers'

Content Knowledge (another strand) forward. In other words, teacher educators can help preservice teachers move forward in their understanding of the content in a discipline, but when they also value and take into account the knowledge and belief of preservice teachers, they can help those preservice teachers move their practices forward in powerful ways. In this light, preservice teachers bring with them their long experience as students and they often value the practices that were used to educate them that do not necessarily promote learning. Teacher educators face the challenging task of helping these students understand new ways of teaching the content.

From this study, then, the strand of *Knowledge and Belief of Preservice Teachers* is critical as teacher educators build curriculum for preservice teachers. Teacher educators need to know not only where their students are–what knowledge they have – but what they believe about it and how they are willing and capable of making curriculum in response. Since teacher educators are often aware that taking up knowledge in a course likely will include preservice teachers confronting, reframing, or clinging to preconceived ideas, notions, and experiences, they know that their curriculum must be designed to help preservice teachers shift their beliefs about the content and the pedagogy being taught.

Since I am a teacher educator operating within the tensions present in teacher education, I was positioned to investigate my decisions in reconceptualizing a class I had previously taught in person and now was going to teach online. As I considered the task, I recognized that I needed to meet the same goals I met when I taught students face-to-face, but I needed to do that in an online environment. Coming to understand my decision-making was the best way to develop and contribute new understandings to the concept of teacher educator knowledge. This would include recognizing the obligations and commitments to students, colleagues, communities, and even myself, and the interaction between these commitments and the teacher educator knowledge I held.

CONTEXTS FOR EXPLORING TEACHER EDUCATOR KNOWLEDGE

While there are many contexts in which S-STEP researchers could explore and unveil additional teacher educator knowledge, the idea is to locate sites of study that require the articulation of teacher educators' thought processes and decision-making. Sites such as program review and accreditation, collaborative book study, experiences with tracing the learning of students across a program, all are places where the shifts, decision-making, and reflection are potentially made visible and accessible to analysis by a teacher educator.

Currently, many teacher educators do not have experience as public school teachers, and therefore, their teacher knowledge, which is fundamental for curriculum-making (Connelly & Clandinin, 1988), has an impact on the teacher educator knowledge they hold. In this study of my teacher educator knowledge, I found myself constantly using my teacher knowledge developed in public school teaching. Those, like me, who began our lives as teachers and constantly draw on that knowledge as we develop curriculum and teach in teacher education may develop different understandings of the strands of teacher educator knowledge. Therefore, in this study of my curriculum-making, my teacher knowledge resides as subtext within all the strands of teacher educator knowledge identified and defined in this study. Since knowledge gained as a teacher, or teacher knowledge, is an important contributor to the knowledge of the teacher educator, teacher educator knowledge is positioned differently. It is more complicated and has more variables. Teacher educators have to use their teacher knowledge to design curriculum for teaching the content of teacher education, whether it be reading, biological sciences, physical education, etc. In addition, a teacher educator needs to design curriculum that will move forward not just the content knowledge of preservice teachers, but also their teacher knowledge (including pedagogical knowledge), which is a more complicated task and for which teacher knowledge forms an important base (Clandinin, 2000).

Central in the context of this study was the process of moving a course that I had often taught face to face, and with which various issues of teacher knowledge were already operating, to an online class. This shift was the perfect site for capturing decisions made and data generated around those decisions. Indeed, this shift provided an ideal situation under which teacher educator knowledge could be uncovered. Like much self-study research, my position as a person making decisions and implementing them became important because externally another person might not be able to see into my thinking – the reasoning behind decisions and what the activities and lessons already designed revealed about what I knew as a teacher educator (Pinnegar & Hamilton, 2009).

Another aspect of the context related to the timing of the study included a concern that in light of the accelerated shift from in-person to online teaching brought on by the COVID-19 pandemic, much of what teacher educators knew about creating optimal curriculum for preservice teachers could be lost in the rush and in the challenge of delivering teacher education in an online format. In the environment of mandated online teacher education, in which teacher educators were expected to easily and quickly transfer their knowledge of preparing preservice teachers to an online context, the research community needed to be able to articulate the teacher educator knowledge that was most efficacious as they adapted or designed their courses to online formats. As mentioned previously, the research community does not have detailed or codified accounts of this kind of knowledge (Vanassche & Berry, 2020). By uncovering, describing, and considering the various components of teacher educator knowledge that emerged in the shift to providing teacher education online, I hoped to make a contribution to the research conversation on teacher educator knowledge in teacher education.

REVISITING THE STRANDS IN RELATION TO THE CONTRIBUTION OF TEACHER EDUCATOR KNOWLEDGE

In a framework of relational teacher education, both the teacher educator and the preservice teacher have obligations and contributions to make in promoting the success of preservice teacher learning (Kitchen, 2005). Pedagogical practices that teacher educators expect preservice teachers to use in their future practice must be experienced and modeled during teacher education coursework, in particular those practices that will "draw forward students' own experiences as a basis for building on and developing their knowledge, skills, and dispositions and generating knowledge in preparation to be teachers" (Cutri, Whiting, & Bybee, 2020, p. 55).

Teacher educators occupy an unusual space in andragogy. Successful teaching approaches for adults for children are not necessarily the same, and yet often teacher candidates are being taught effective pedagogy for children and adolescents by teacher educators in an adult classroom setting. Indeed, it can be a difficult challenge for teacher educators to model instruction that will be effective with young learners in a classroom of adults, and in the past, has resulted in teacher education that relied on a delivery system of just telling preservice teachers what is best to do (Loughran & Hamilton, 2016). In this study, I wrestled with the project-based structure of the class and other assignments designed to model and support language and literacy growth for their future learners while also including in the design those strategies and learning engagement opportunities that I believed would help draw forward their own experiences as they simultaneously developed their teacher knowledge, skills, and dispositions. I wanted to give a careful accounting of those teacher education practices particularly attuned to changing preservice teacher belief and disposition that are important for supporting teacher educators as they engage in curriculum-making for teacher education. As indicated, I recognized that as I shifted from in-person to online teaching, the tacit knowledge behind the knowledge I held as a teacher educator to do this would become more visible. The research question that guided my study as set forth in Chapter 1 was, "What does my transition to online teaching reveal about my teacher educator knowledge?"

This study was undertaken as a self-study of teacher education practice in order to both improve my own practice in the move to online teaching and uncover understandings or strands of teacher educator knowledge. Since much of teacher educator knowledge is tacit and embodied, it only becomes obvious as we document decisions or reflection (Polanyi, 2009). I chose to engage in a self-study of practice during a shift in practice, since such shifts in practice are often successful points of discovery for making visible what we know (Pinnegar & Hamilton, 2009). During the spring of 2020 in the midst of the COVID-19 pandemic and at an institution of higher education, I was preparing to teach a course to preservice teachers supporting them in integrating content and promoting language and literacy for English learners in whatever content they were teaching. At the end of winter semester of 2020, all students were sent home to their permanent addresses, and were unable to attend classes in person or visit public school classrooms through spring term. In this context, I took up a study of my own teacher educator knowledge.

The reason for choosing self-study of practice as a methodological stance and the qualitative strategies I employed to explore my practice were outlined in Chapter 3. The study of one's own practice as a teacher educator positions the researcher with an inherent need to immediately implement any new understandings that come from the research project. It also positions the researcher with an obligation to articulate those understandings in a way that can contribute to the larger research conversation (LaBoskey, 2004). The purposes and characteristics of this study aligned with LaBoskey's (2004) assertions about S-STEP. Further, the purposes and characteristics of this study answered Zeichner's (2005) call to educational researchers to engage in more investigation of teacher educators themselves. Since teacher educator knowledge is an emerging field and most research findings concerning it have been captured through S-STEP inquiries (Vanassche & Berry, 2020), this was the methodology used in this study.

In order to make visible my tacit knowledge, I took up the opportunity to examine my teacher educator knowledge as I engaged in decisions about content, curriculum design, implementation, and instruction of a course I had often taught before in person. Therefore, the purpose of this study was to explore teacher educator knowledge as I, interacting with a critical friend, moved from curriculum-making for in-person courses to curriculum-making for an online course. Because I was building on a course I had already taught in person and as I made decisions about the important activities, content knowledge, and experiences students would have in an online setting, it also made visible earlier decisions I had made in building this course for an in-person delivery. Through the gathering of data and interactions with a critical friend during planning, teaching, and reflecting on the course, I was able to explore more comprehensively my teacher educator knowledge.

Because of the complexity and volume of data, in order to support the strands of teacher educator knowledge I was asserting, I composed three analytic narrative vignettes in order to analyze and represent particular strands of teacher educator knowledge that had emerged in ongoing data collection and analysis. As I unpacked my data, I began to see the ways the strands were interrelated and interacted with each other in my decision-making and reflecting process. Other qualitative strategies such as critical friendship, dialogue as a tool in self-study research, and analytic narrative vignettes were essential in my analysis and are discussed in Chapter 3, which includes detailed descriptions of the data collection and analysis methods. This thorough accounting acted to establish a qualitative researcher's transparency and trustworthiness during the study.

In Chapter 4, I discussed the principles and practices that guided me in the construction of analytic narrative vignettes. I explained various benefits of the use of exemplars to represent large quantities of text within narrative accounts. In particular, such exemplars can capture the three-dimensional narrative space (Clandinin & Connelly, 2000), giving narrative texture and sense to the time, place, and participants of a study. Since my study was a close-up and personal accounting of one period of time as a teacher educator, the composition of vignettes helped capture the particular details, challenges, and thinking that occurred during that time and allowed me a way to manageably express the experience. In the process of making the vignettes, I also found that they provided a secure space from which I could confidently make assertions about the strands and their interactions with each other. In fact, they supported further analysis,

EXPLORING TEACHER EDUCATOR KNOWLEDGE 119

giving insight about how the strands of teacher educator knowledge resonated while allowing my accounts to remain situated in the context and the relationships. Because of these benefits, the process of capturing themes (strands) occurred as I was planning, teaching, and reflecting on the course and was revealed through dialogue and other field notes. In composing and unpacking the analytic narrative vignettes further, the trustworthiness was increased.

The seven strands of teacher educator knowledge emerged from the data, the construction of narrative vignettes, and in the ongoing analysis of both. The findings emerged in the data during the planning, teaching, and reflecting on the course. These strands of teacher educator knowledge were identified as I analyzed the data gathered and then used for composing three analytic narrative vignettes (Erickson, 1986; Miles et al., 2018). Again, as explained in Chapter 4, the three vignettes, one representing each phase (Planning, Teaching, Reflecting), captured the seven strands of teacher educator knowledge and their interactions in decision-making.

All seven strands were present in each narrative vignette and were unpacked, defined, and explicated in context of the vignettes in Chapters 5–7. The seven strands that emerged as relevant teacher educator knowledge were *Content Knowledge, Fixed and Fluid Elements, Knowledge of Milieu, Pedagogical Intent, Preservice Teacher Knowledge and Belief, Theory Matters*, and *Value and Fragility of Relationships.*

In fact, in Chapter 5, the Planning Vignette revealed that the strands of teacher educator knowledge were evident from the beginning. For example, from the first meetings about shifting the course online, our dialogue revealed discussions of *Fixed and Fluid Elements* as we tried to determine how to run class so that students knew what to expect and would be willing to work on the somewhat ambiguous and challenging assignment of working in a small group over Zoom to design real activities for elementary aged students. This planning led me to consider how in the past, class sessions were very different, some being really content-heavy, filled with readings and activities, and other sessions given over as completely to students as work sessions. It became clear to me during planning that there was perhaps a different, more routine way to proceed with class that would make class time feel less uncertain to students. The other strands were also relevant in the Planning Vignette. Others were just as relevant as the one discussed here but not as obviously referred to. More insights from the Planning Vignette were discussed in detail in Chapter 5.

The Teaching Vignette revealed that strands of teacher educator knowledge became more visible when I taught the online course. For example, the vignette captured the beginning of the first session teaching over Zoom, with teacher introductions, and later, the experience of working with groups in breakout rooms. My spoken dialogue with students revealed my beliefs about *Content Knowledge, Theory Matters*, and *Value and Fragility of Relationships* as I encouraged students to notice how the class was designed in ways I wanted them to work with their students and underscored the importance of relationships. It was significant that the strands were often very tightly intertwined while teaching, with more than one strand in play at any given time. As an additional example, my constant attention to how well groups were collaborating emphasized my understanding of *Content Knowledge*, the value I placed on matters of *Theory*, and the frequent concern and attention I gave to the *Value and Fragility of Relationships*. More insights from the Teaching Vignette were analyzed and presented in Chapter 6.

In the Reflecting Vignette, I represented the data gathered after teaching, including debriefing meetings that occurred immediately following a class session and the final reflections engaged in after the course was over. At this point, the strands were solidified and robust. For example, the strand of *Pedagogical Intent* had emerged immediately during the planning of the course and helped guide my teaching in the moment, but in moments of reflection, this knowledge, of how to design activities with learning outcomes in mind, had me naturally examining my course decisions, my teaching, perceptions, interactions, and outcomes.

Indeed, I realized while reflecting on the course that attention to *Pedagogical Intent*, whether or not activities were meeting their learning purposes, allowed me to simultaneously attend to *Content Knowledge, Fixed and Fluid Elements, Knowledge of Milieu, Preservice Teacher Knowledge and Belief*, and *Theory* – basically connecting to all the other strands. Other insights from the Reflecting Vignette were analyzed and presented in Chapter 7.

In Chapter 8, the discussion was guided by the research question that steered my study, "What does my transition to online teaching reveal about my teacher educator knowledge?" I realized that the seven strands of teacher educator knowledge that emerged during the shift to teaching an online course deserved a more in-depth explanation. According to Connelly et al. (1997), teacher knowledge and knowing has a direct impact on all areas and aspects of the teaching act. This assertion would seem to be the same for teacher educator knowledge action and knowing. As I turned to each of the seven strands of teacher educator knowledge, I recognized how my definitions, exemplars, and perspectives were thoroughly situated in my own tacit, moral, social, and relational context (Vanassche & Berry, 2020).

In Chapter 8, in order to reach for deeper understanding of the strands, I attended to each strand individually, providing a more specific discussion of each strand and how its presence and nuanced variability in planning, teaching, or reflecting allowed a more complex representation of the strand. Part of that nuance and complexity was in how the strands varied based on which context they occurred in (Planning, Teaching, Reflecting). I defined and explained the strands of teacher educator knowledge more holistically as a way of turning my newly articulated thinking back to my own practice in an online context and then turning my knowledge outward to inform the larger research community about teacher educator knowledge more generally (LaBoskey, 2004).

As I took up the discussion of each strand, I recognized that I had made certain commitments to preservice teachers that I also included in my discussion of teacher educator knowledge. As LaBoskey (2004) suggests, understandings that are uncovered by teacher educators in relationship to practices become a source of motivation and a commitment to improving practice based on what was learned. This is because the ultimate obligation as teacher educators is not merely to the preservice teachers they teach, but to their students as well (Arizona Group, 1997).

In conclusion, the investigation of my own teacher educator knowledge conducted during an intentional shift in my practice and curriculum-making was a rich context for such exploration. This inquiry included the work of collecting the data, engaging in dialogue with my critical friend, identifying and examining the emerging and interwoven strands of teacher educator knowledge, and engaging in further analysis through the use of exemplars in the form of analytic narrative vignettes. This process allowed me to make more explicit the tacit knowledge I held as a teacher educator. However, as Polanyi (2009) argues, as soon as we extract tacit knowledge and make it visible, it folds back into the tacit knowledge guiding our actions. In this way, this characteristic of tacit knowledge makes ongoing self-study of practice fresh and new with each study. What also becomes visible in this study is the way that the strands of teacher educator knowledge are entangled and evolving. Polanyi (2009) also suggests that as we use tacit knowledge and pay attention to it, learning occurs and the knowledge or practice under study grows and evolves.

WHAT ARE THE IMPLICATIONS OF STUDIES OF TEACHER EDUCATOR KNOWLEDGE FOR TEACHER EDUCATION?

ABSTRACT

Rather than a stance of knowledge for teachers (Clandinin, 2000), the strands of teacher educator knowledge are rooted in an orientation of what teacher educators know and are well positioned to contribute to the research conversation in teacher education. The strands of teacher educator knowledge are interconnected and can help guide teacher educators' practice in curriculum planning and decision-making. In this study, I found that all the strands informed each other and were tightly related; therefore, it would be helpful to understand the interplay between different aspects of teacher educator knowledge, which are more fundamental, and what other strands would emerge. Since my understanding of these strands of teacher educator knowledge was situated my own complex, tacit, moral and relational context, it would also be beneficial for other teacher educators to identify and express their own teacher educator knowledge, so that other possibilities and perspectives on teacher educator knowledge could be conceptualized and deeper, more nuanced definitions expressed. This chapter examines guiding ideas for future research and potential sites for future research into teacher educator knowledge. Implications for practitioners are also explored. As this study made clear, it could be helpful if teacher educators attended to the ethical concerns they hold for their students, themselves, and their colleagues in their practice. Such concerns are made visible when teacher educators consider their own knowledge in the various sites mentioned that can reveal tacit knowledge.

Keywords: Teacher educator knowledge; tacit knowledge; teacher education; self-study of practice; trustworthiness; narrative research; moral dimensions; ethical concerns; teacher knowledge; online education

---

Exploring Teacher Educator Knowledge
Advances in Research on Teaching, Volume 48, 123–127
Copyright © 2025 Celina Dulude Lay
Published under exclusive licence by Emerald Publishing Limited
ISSN: 1479-3687/doi:10.1108/S1479-368720240000048010

GUIDING FUTURE RESEARCH

Exploration of teacher educator knowledge is still in its infancy. Teacher education courses and programs often fall into the trap described by Clandinin (2000) where she argues that most teacher education programs focus on knowledge for teaching, which allows for the knowledge needed for preservice teachers and practicing teachers to be segmented and portioned into pieces as courses and standards and practices. Such an approach leaves teacher educators out of the loop as preservice teachers then have the responsibility to integrate that knowledge. Her account of teacher educator programs which are designed from a basis of teacher knowledge recognize the holistic quality of teacher knowledge. From the beginning of teacher preparation, preservice teachers come to the program with knowledge from their own experiences in schooling. Indeed, they have already begun to develop teacher knowledge.

At the institution where I teach, the preservice teachers not only come with their past experience as students but have also often had practice as piano teachers, swim coaches, dance instructors, course TA's in high school, choir directors, served as volunteer missionaries, and had teaching experiences of all kinds where they were positioned as teacher. What the concept of knowledge of teaching suggests is that preservice teachers come to teaching from many paths, and those paths will influence the knowledge and practices that they understand and take up in their own teaching. Most teacher education programs do acknowledge that preservice teachers come with knowledge of teaching, but then immediately ignore it. Many programs seem unable to build on and expand that preservice teacher knowledge or identify where their experiences and knowledge as teachers may contradict or be in opposition to what the program would like them to do. Knowledge of teaching, like the strands of teacher educator knowledge, are intertwined with each other and guide practice in curriculum planning and decision-making. Therefore, teacher educator knowledge could make an important contribution and needs to be studied further.

POTENTIAL SITES FOR FUTURE RESEARCH ON TEACHER EDUCATOR KNOWLEDGE

Further investigations into teacher educator knowledge could explore the strands of teacher educator knowledge in studies that looked at field experiences and placements, as well as other in-person and online contexts. For example, in this study, context was important with some strands being especially valuable for carrying out the goals and purposes of the course *(Pedagogical Intent)*. In this study, we found teacher educator knowledge of *Fixed and Fluid Elements* was potentially even more important in online rather than in-person contexts since teacher educators must make many informed decisions about a course in advance in order to tailor curriculum and open space in the moment of teaching to support preservice teachers in their learning. Thus, explorations into how the strands

EXPLORING TEACHER EDUCATOR KNOWLEDGE

of teacher educator knowledge are enacted in online settings as well as in other school-based and field-based settings would be useful.

Profitable sites for future studies of teacher educator knowledge include any situation where shifts in teacher educator knowledge would occur. Some of these would include experiences in supervising field experiences, program development, course or assignment design or redesign, examination of former students' current practices, etc. Other sites for study might include changes in experience such as returning from sabbatical, achieving tenure or full professor, being involved in accreditation, observing the teaching of other teacher educators, etc.

Because teacher education is fundamentally relational, moral and ethical concerns are always present. Therefore, explorations into the ways in which moral and ethical concerns shape and constrain teacher educator knowledge could lead to a deeper and more nuanced understanding of how the moral and ethical are involved in teacher educator knowledge and decision-making. In a sense, looking at these situations is another site for study.

This study uncovered my teacher educator knowledge. I was raised by teachers, and I bring to teacher education my experience and knowledge as a preservice teacher prepared in a university-based program, experienced in teaching in public school and in a private residential treatment center setting. I currently work as an adjunct teacher educator, educational researcher, and curriculum maker. However, other teacher educators bring different backgrounds and are engaged in curriculum-making in teacher education in vastly different contexts. Studies that uncover their teacher educator knowledge can build on this study and contribute to the research conversation in teacher education as well as understandings of knowledge as a teacher educator.

Also, in this study, I found that all the strands informed each other and were tightly related; therefore, it would be helpful to understand the interplay between different aspects of teacher educator knowledge, which are more fundamental, and what other strands would emerge. Since my understanding of these strands of teacher educator knowledge was situated my own complex, tacit, moral and relational context, it would also be beneficial for other teacher educators to identify and express their own teacher educator knowledge, so that other possibilities and perspectives on teacher educator knowledge could be conceptualized and deeper, more nuanced definitions expressed.

IMPLICATIONS FOR PRACTITIONERS

The positioning of teacher education within institutions of higher education, differences in approach to educating preservice teachers and between university coursework and field experiences are inherent tensions that teacher educators live with. Despite these continuing tensions, teacher educators can choose to thrive in these environments (Berry, 2007). As teacher educators are more aware of their knowledge, I wonder how this would shift their practice. An understanding of teacher educator knowledge may also help teacher educators grapple with the complexity of teaching teachers to be student-centered and resisting "do as I say, not as I do" approaches to teacher education (Kimmons, personal communication, November 2020). Indeed, articulated understandings of teacher educator knowledge may reveal those commitments and associated practices for supporting preservice teachers (Kitchen, 2020). By recognizing and naming their teacher educator knowledge, teacher educators can sharpen and improve their practice as they design courses, including improvements in online teacher education, participate in constructing programs, and defend their programs in accreditation processes.

As this study made clear, it would be helpful if teacher educators attended to the ethical concerns they hold for their students, themselves, and their colleagues in their practice. Such concerns are made visible when teacher educators consider their own knowledge in the various sites mentioned that can reveal tacit knowledge. Further, they need to attend to moral concerns for institutions and scholarly communities of teacher education as well as the students their preservice teachers will teach (Pinnegar & Murphy, 2019). As they develop understanding of their knowledge and its entanglement, they are more able to align their action with their moral and ethical concerns.

Additionally, teacher educator knowledge has important implications and applications for in-service teacher professional development. Teacher educators need to utilize models such as PICRAT that enable them to critique and improve their attention to technology and its uses in their courses, particularly online courses (Kimmons et al., 2020). It would be important to see how teacher educator knowledge may apply to the development of teacher professional learning programs and avenues of support for practicing teachers. Those involved in ongoing professional learning are often entrenched in their perspectives and their knowledge as teachers, but research on teacher educator knowledge could support those involved in teacher education and teacher professional development to identify their own teacher educator knowledge and help them grow as teacher educators.

CONCLUSION

This study added to the growing conceptualization of teacher educator knowledge as a complex, broad, personal, tacit, and situated body of knowledge that also ties together knowledge of subject matter, pedagogical skills, preservice teacher knowledge and belief and is situated in a moral stance of obligation to unseen children (Arizona Group, 1997; Dewey, 1929/2013; Vanassche & Berry, 2020). Teacher educators enact their teacher educator knowledge to design learning experiences with the goal not of transferring their own knowledge but of supporting preservice teachers shape and reshape knowledge they already have (Clandinin, 2000).

This study underscored the importance of relationship building, preservice teacher beliefs, engagement with preservice teachers and with the content, and a core attention to theory, especially a deep theoretical knowledge of sociocultural learning, learning online and using technology, and the interplay of Schwab's (1973) commonplaces of teacher, student, milieu, and subject matter in action. In this narrative self-study of teacher practice, the work of uncovering teacher educator knowledge revealed theoretical bases and pedagogical intent behind instructional decisions and provided new strategies for analyzing pedagogy, interactions with preservice teachers, and curriculum. The descriptions of teacher educator knowledge described in this study, though particular to one researcher, revealed obligations to preservice teachers that assisted this researcher in the process of planning, teaching, and reflecting on an online course. These identified strands of teacher educator knowledge helped the researcher specify knowledge essential in supporting preservice teacher learning and make evident important obligations and commitments.

REFERENCES

Abu El-Haj, T. R., & Rubin, B. C. (2009). Realizing the equity-minded aspirations of detracking and inclusion: Toward a capacity-oriented framework for teacher education. *Curriculum Inquiry*, *39*(3), 435–463. https://doi.org/10.1111/j.1467-873X.2009.00451.x

Allen, I. E., & Seaman, J. (2013). *Changing course: Ten years of tracking online education in the United States.* Sloan Consortium.

Allman, B., & Pinnegar, S. E. (2020). A self-study of aligning pedagogy with technology in online course design. In C. U. Edge, A. Cameron-Standerford, & B. Bergh (Eds.), *Textiles and tapestries: Self-study for envisioning new ways of knowing.* EdTech Books. https://edtechbooks.org/textiles_tapestries_self_study/chapter_2

Altenbaugh, R. J., & Underwood, K. (1990). The evolution of normal schools. In J. I. Goodlad, R. Soder, & K. A. Sirotnik (Eds.), *Places where teachers are taught* (pp. 136–186). Jossey-Boss.

American Association of Colleges for Teacher Education. (2013). *The changing teacher preparation profession: A report from AACTE's professional education data system (PEDS).* https://secure.aacte.org/apps/rl/res_get.php?fid=145&ref=rl

Arizona Group. (1995). Becoming teachers of teachers: Alternative paths expressed in beginners' voices. In F., Korthagen & T., Russell (Eds.), *Teachers who teach teachers: Reflections on teacher education* (pp. 35–55). Falmer Press.

Arizona Group. (1997). Obligations to unseen children. In J., Loughran & T., Russell (Eds.), *Teaching about teaching: Purpose, passion, and pedagogy in teacher education* (pp. 183–209). Falmer Press.

Arum, R., & Stevens, M. L. (2020, March 18). What is a college education in the time of coronavirus? *The New York Times.* https://www.nytimes.com/2020/03/18/opinion/college-education-coronavirus.html. Accessed on February 23, 2021.

Ball, D. L., & Forzani, F. M. (2009). The work of teaching and the challenge for teacher education. *Journal of Teacher Education, 60*(5), 497–511. https://doi.org/10.1177%2F0022487109348479

Berry, A. (2007). *Tensions in teaching about teaching: Understanding practice as a teacher educator* (Vol. 5). Springer Science & Business Media.

Berry, A., Depaepe, F., & van Driel, J. (2016). Pedagogical content knowledge in teacher education. In J. Loughran & M. L. Hamilton (Eds.), *International handbook of teacher education* (pp. 347–386). Springer.

Borko, H., Jacobs, J., & Koellner, K. (2010). Contemporary approaches to teacher professional development. *International Encyclopedia of Education, 7*(2), 548–556.

Boy, J., Rensink, R. A., Bertini, E., & Fekete, J. D. (2014). A principled way of assessing visualization literacy. *IEEE Transactions on Visualization and Computer Graphics, 20*(12), 1963–1972.

Brookfield, S. D. (2017). *Becoming a critically reflective teacher.* John Wiley & Sons.

Brown, T., Rowley, H., & Smith, K. (2016). Sliding subject positions: Knowledge and teacher educators. *British Educational Research Journal, 42*(3), 492–507.

Bullock, S. M. (2017). Understanding candidates' learning relationships with their cooperating teachers: A call to reframe my pedagogy. *Studying Teacher Education, 13*(2), 179–192. https://doi.org/10.1080/17425964.2017.1342355

Bullock, S. M., & Fletcher, T. (2017). Teaching about teaching using technology: Using embodiment to interpret online pedagogies of teacher education. In D. Garbett & A. Ovens (Eds.), *Being self-study researchers in a digital world. Self-study of teaching and teacher education practices* (Vol. 16). Springer. https://doi.org/10.1007/978-3-319-39478-7_3

Bullock, S. M., & Ritter, J. K. (2011). Exploring the transition into academia through collaborative self-study. *Studying Teacher Education, 7*(2), 171–181.

130 REFERENCES

Bullough, R. V., Jr., & Stokes, D. K. (1994). Analyzing personal teaching metaphors in preservice teacher education as a means for encouraging professional development. *American Educational Research Journal, 31*(1), 191–224. https://doi.org/10.3102/00028312031001197

Bullough, R. V., Jr. (2019). *Essays on teaching education and the inner drama of teaching: Where troubles meet issues* (Vol. 32). Emerald Publishing Limited. https://doi.org/10.1108/S1479-368720190000032001

Bullough, R. V., Jr. Clark, D. C., & Patterson, R. S. (2003). Getting in step: Accountability, accreditation, and the standardization of teacher education in the Unites States. *Journal of Education for Teaching, 29*(1), 35–51. https://doi.org/10.1080/0260747022000057945

Bullough, R. V., Jr. Knowles, J. G., & Crow, N. A. (1991). *Emerging as a teacher.* Taylor & Francis.

Burbank, M. D., Kauchak, D., & Bates, A. J. (2010). Book clubs as professional development opportunities for preservice teacher candidates and practicing teachers: An exploratory study. *The New Educator, 6*(1), 56–73. https://files.eric.ed.gov/fulltext/EJ893563.pdf

Bussmann, S., Johnson, S. R., Oliver, R., Forsythe, K., Grandjean, M., Lebsock, M., & Luster, T. (2017). On the recognition of quality online course design in promotion and tenure: A survey of higher ed institutions in the western United States. *Online Journal of Distance Learning Administration, 20*(1).

Chick, H., & Beswick, K. (2018). Teaching teachers to teach Boris: A framework for mathematics teacher educator pedagogical content knowledge. *Journal of Mathematics Teacher Education, 21*(5), 475–499. https://doi.org/10.1007/s10857-016-9362-y

Clandinin, D. J. (2000). Learning to teach: A question of knowledge. *Education Canada, 40*, 28–30.

Clandinin, D. J., & Connelly, F. M. (2000). *Narrative inquiry: Experience and story in qualitative research.* Jossey-Bass.

Clandinin, D. J., Davies, A., Hogan, P., & Kennard, B. (1993). *Learning to teach, teaching to learn: Stories of collaboration in teacher education.* Teachers College Press.

Clandinin, D. J., Downey, C. A., & Huber, J. (2009). Attending to changing landscapes: Shaping our identities as teacher educators. *Asia-Pacific Journal of Teacher Education, 37*(2), 141–154. https://doi.org/10.1080/13598660902806316

Clandinin, D. J., & Husu, J. (Eds.). (2017). *The SAGE handbook of research on teacher education.* Sage.

Clifford, G. J., & Guthrie, J. W. (1990). *Ed school: A brief for professional education.* University of Chicago Press.

Clift, R. T., & Brady, P. (2005). Research on methods courses and field experiences. In M. Cochran-Smith & K. Zeichner (Eds.), *Studying teacher education: The report of the AERA panel on research and teacher education* (pp. 309–424). Lawrence Erlbaum.

Cochran-Smith, M., & Fries, K. (2005). The AERA panel on research and teacher education: Context and goals. In M. Cochran-Smith & K. Zeichner (Eds.), *Studying teacher education: The report of the AERA panel on research and teacher education* (pp. 37–68). Lawrence Erlbaum.

Cochran-Smith, M. & Zeichner, K. (Eds.). (2005). *Studying teacher education: The report of the AERA panel on research and teacher education.* Lawrence Erlbaum.

Connelly, F. M., & Clandinin, D. J. (1988). *Teachers as curriculum planners. Narratives of experience.* Teachers College Press.

Connelly, F. M., Clandinin, D. J., & He, M. F. (1997). Teachers' personal practical knowledge on the professional knowledge landscape. *Teaching and Teacher Education, 13*(7), 665–674. https://doi.org/10.1016/S0742-051X(97)00014-0

Craig, C. J. (2008). Joseph Schwab, self-study of teaching and teacher education practices proponent? A personal perspective. *Teaching and Teacher Education, 24*(8), 1993–2001. https://doi.org/10.1016/j.tate.2008.05.008

Cutri, R. M., & Mena, J. (2020). A critical reconceptualization of faculty readiness for online teaching. *Distance Education, 41*(3), 361–380. https://doi.org/10.1080/01587919.2020.1763167

Cutri, R. M., Mena, J., & Whiting, E. F. (2020). Faculty readiness for online crisis teaching: Transitioning to online teaching during the COVID-19 pandemic. *European Journal of Teacher Education, 43*(4), 523–541. https://doi.org/10.1080/02619768.2020.1815702

Cutri, R. M., & Whiting, E. F. (2018). Opening spaces for teacher educator knowledge in a faculty development program on blended learning course development. *Studying Teacher Education, 14*(2), 125–140. https://doi.org/10.1080/17425964.2018.1447920

References

131

Cutri, R. M., Whiting, E. F., & Bybee, E. R. (2020). Knowledge production and power in an online critical multicultural teacher education course. *Educational Studies*, *56*(1), 54–65. https://doi.org/10.1080/00131946.2019.1645016

Dahal, N., & Pangeni, S. K. (2019). in online courses: Insights for learning and assessment in higher education. *International Journal of Multidisciplinary Perspectives in Higher Education*, *4*(1), 89–110.

Darling-Hammond, L. (2004). "Steady work": The ongoing redesign of the Stanford Teacher Education Program. *Educational Perspectives*, *36*(1–2), 8–19. https://files.eric.ed.gov/fulltext/EJ877594.pdf

Darling-Hammond, L. (2006). Constructing 21st-century teacher education. *Journal of Teacher Education*, *57*(3), 300–314. https://doi.org/10.1177/0022487105285962

Darling-Hammond, L., Hyler, M. E., & Gardner, M. (2017). *Effective teacher professional development*. Learning Policy Institute. https://learningpolicyinstitute.org/product/effective-teacher%02professional-development-report

Davey, R. (2013). *The professional identity of teacher educators: Career on the cusp?*. Routledge.

de Kramer, R. M., Masters, J., O'Dwyer, L., Dash, S., & Russell, M. (2012). Relationship of online teacher professional development to seventh-grade teachers' and students' knowledge and practices in English language arts. *The Teacher Educator*, *47*(3), 236–259. http://doi.org/10.1080/08878730.2012.685795

Dede, C., Jass Ketelhut, D., Whitehouse, P., Breit, L., & McCloskey, E. M. (2009). A research agenda for online teacher professional development. *Journal of Teacher Education*, *60*(1), 8–19. https://doi.org/10.1177%2F0022487108327554

Dell, C. A., Hobbs, S. F., & Miller, K. (2008). Effective online teacher preparation: Lessons learned. *MERLOT Journal of Online Learning and Teaching*, *4*(4), 602–610.

Depaepe, F., Verschaffel, L., & Kelchtermans, G. (2013). Pedagogical content knowledge: A systematic review of the way in which the concept has pervaded mathematics educational research. *Teaching and Teacher Education*, *34*, 12–25.

Desimone, L. M. (2009). Improving impact studies of teachers' professional development: Toward better conceptualizations and measures. *Educational Researcher*, *38*(3), 181–199. https://doi.org/10.3102%2F0013189X08331140

Dewey, J. (2007). Logic: The theory of inquiry. In J. A. Boydston (Ed.), *The Later Works, 1925-1953* (Vol. 12). Southern Illinois Press. (Original work published 1938)

Dewey, J. (2013). *The sources of a science of education*. The Daniel Tanner Foundation. (Original work published 1929)

Dintersmith, T. (2018). *What school could be*. Princeton University Press.

Downing, J. J., & Dyment, J. E. (2013). Teacher educators' readiness, preparation, and perceptions of preparing preservice teachers in a fully online environment: An exploratory study. *The Teacher Educator*, *48*(2), 96–109. https://doi.org/10.1080/08878730.2012.760023

Doyle, W. (1990). Themes in teacher education research. In W. R. Houston, M. Haberman, & J. Sikula (Eds.), *Handbook of research on teacher education* (pp. 3–24). Macmillan.

Ducharme, E., & Ducharme, M. (1996). Needed research in teacher education. In J. Sikula (Ed.), *Handbook of research on teacher education* (pp. 1030–1046). Macmillan.

Dyment, J. E., & Downing, J. J. (2020). Online initial teacher education: A systematic review of the literature. *Asia-Pacific Journal of Teacher Education*, *48*(3), 316–333. https://doi.org/10.1080/1359866X.2019.1631254

Echevarria, J., Vogt, M., & Short, D. (2012). *Making content comprehensible for English Language Learners: The SIOP model* (4th ed.). Pearson.

Erickson, F. (1986). Qualitative methods in research on teaching. In M. Wittrock (Ed.), *Handbook of research on teaching* (pp. 119–161). Macmillan.

Fazio, X., Melville, W., & Bartley, A. (2010). The problematic nature of the practicum: A key determinant of pre-service teachers' emerging inquiry-based science practices. *Journal of Science Teacher Education*, *21*(6), 665–681. https://doi.org/10.1007/s10972-010-9209-9

Fenstermacher, G. D. (1994). The knower and the known: The nature of knowledge in research on teaching. *Review of Research in Education*, *20*(1), 3–56.

Ferdig, R. E., Baumgartner, E., Hartshorne, R., Kaplan-Rakowski, R., & Mouza, C. (2020). *Teaching, technology, and teacher education during the COVID-19 pandemic: Stories from the field*. Association for the Advancement of Computing in Education (AACE). https://www.learntechlib.org/p/216903/

132 REFERENCES

Fletcher, T., Ní Chróinín, D., Price, C., & Francis, N. (2018). Teacher educators' enactment of pedagogies that prioritise learning about meaningful physical education. *Curriculum Studies in Health and Physical Education, 9*(1), 76–89. https://doi.org/10.1080/18377122.2018.1425125

Gage, N. L. (1972). *Teacher effectiveness and teacher education: The search for a scientific basis.* Pacific Books.

Garbett, D. (2013). Promotion by teaching distinction: Developing resilience and cache for a track less traveled. *Studying Teacher Education, 9*(2), 108–117. https://doi.org/10.1080/17425964.2013.808045

Garrison, D. R., Anderson, T., & Archer, W. (2004). Critical thinking, cognitive presence, and computer conferencing in distance education. *American Journal of Distance Education, 13*(1), 57–75. http://doi.org/10.1080/08923640109527071

Glaser, B. G., & Strauss, A. L. (2017). *Discovery of grounded theory: Strategies for qualitative research.* Routledge. (Originally published, 1967)

Goodlad, J. I. (1984). *A place called school: Prospects for the future.* McGraw-Hill.

Goodlad, J. I. (1990a). *Teachers for our nation's schools.* Jossey-Bass.

Goodlad, J. I. (1990b). The occupation of teaching in schools. In J. I. Goodlad, R. Soder, & K. A. Sirotnik (Eds.), *The moral dimensions of teaching* (pp. 3–34). Jossey-Bass.

Goodlad, J. I., Soder, R., & Sirotnik, K. A. (Eds.). (1990). *Places where teachers are taught.* Jossey-Bass.

Grant, K. S. L., Lee, V. J., & Lyttle, C. F. (2018). White preservice and inservice teachers' engagement with multicultural content in online courses. *Multicultural Education, 26*(1), 17–23.

Grossman, P. L. (1992). Why models matter: An alternative view on professional growth in teaching. *Review of Educational Research, 62*(2), 171–179. https://doi.org/10.3102%2F003465 43062002171

Grossman, P. (2018). *Teaching core practices in teacher education.* Harvard Education Press.

Grossman, P., & Shulman, L. (1994). Knowing, believing, and the teaching of English. In T. Shanahan (Ed.), *Teachers thinking, teachers knowing: Reflections on literacy and language education* (pp. 3–16). National Council of Teachers of English.

Hadar, L. L., & Brody, D. L. (2017). Professional learning and development of teacher educators. In J. Clandinin & J. Husu (Eds.), *The SAGE handbook of research on teacher education* (Vol. 2, pp. 1049–1064). Sage.

Hambacher, E., Ginn, K., & Slater, K. (2018). Letting students lead: Preservice teachers' experiences of learning in online discussions. *Journal of Digital Learning in Teacher Education, 34*(3), 151–165. http://doi.org/10.1080/21532974.2018.1453893

Hamilton, M. L., Hutchinson, D. A., & Pinnegar, S. (2020). Quality, trustworthiness, and S-STTEP research. In J. Kitchen, A. Berry, S. M. Bullock, A. R. Crowe, M. Taylor, H. Guðjónsdóttir, & L. Thomas (Eds.), *International handbook of self-study of teaching and teacher education practices* (pp. 299–338). Springer.

Hamilton, M. L., & Pinnegar, S. (2015). Considering the role of self-study of teaching and teacher education practices research in transforming urban classrooms. *Studying Teacher Education, 11*(2), 180–190. https://doi.org/10.1080/17425964.2015.1045775

Hamilton, M. L., Pinnegar, S., & Davey, R. (2016). Intimate scholarship: An examination of identity and inquiry in the work of teacher educators. In J. Loughran & M. L. Hamilton (Eds.), *International handbook of teacher education* (pp. 181–237). Springer.

Hartshorne, R., Baumgartner, E., Kaplan-Rakowski, R., Mouza, C., & Ferdig, R. E. (2020). Special issue editorial: Preservice and inservice professional development during the COVID-19 pandemic. *Journal of Technology and Teacher Education, 28*(2), 137–147.

Hechinger, J., & Lorin, J. (2020, March 19). *Coronavirus forces $600 billion higher education industry online.* Bloomberg Businessweek. https://www.bloomberg.com/news/articles/2020-03-19/colleges-are-going-online-because-of-the-coronavirus. Accessed on February 23, 2021.

Hew, K. F., & Brush, T. (2007). Integrating technology into K-12 teaching and learning: Current knowledge gaps and recommendations for future research. *Educational Technology Research & Development, 55*(3), 223–252.

References

Hill, H. C., Ball, D. L., & Schilling, S. G. (2008). Unpacking pedagogical content knowledge: Conceptualizing and measuring teachers' topic-specific knowledge of students. *Journal for Research in Mathematics Education, 39*(4), 372–400.

Hodges, C., Moore, S., Lockee, B., Trust, T., & Bond, A. (2020). The difference between emergency remote teaching and online learning. *Educause Review, 27*. https://er.educause.edu/articles/2020/3/the-difference-between-emergency-remote-teaching-and-online-learning

Holt-Reynolds, D. (1991). *Practicing what we teach.* National Center for Research on Teacher Learning, Michigan State University.

Holt-Reynolds, D. (1992). Personal history-based beliefs as relevant prior knowledge in course work. *American Educational Research Journal, 29*(2), 325–349. https://doi.org/10.3102%2F00028312029002325

Hume, A., & Berry, A. (2011). Constructing CoRes—A strategy for building PCK in pre-service science teacher education. *Research in Science Education, 41*(3), 341–355. https://doi.org/10.1007/s11165-010-9168-3

Kagan, D. M. (1992). Professional growth among preservice and beginning teachers. *Review of Educational Research, 62*(2), 129–169. https://doi.org/10.3102%2F00346543062002129

Kennedy, K., & Archambault, L. (2012). Offering preservice teachers field experiences in K-12 online learning: A national survey of teacher education programs. *Journal of Teacher Education, 63*(3), 185–200. https://doi.org/10.1177%2F0022487111433651

Kimmons, R. (2020). Current trends (and missing links) in educational technology research and practice. *TechTrends, 64*, 803–809. https://doi.org/10.1007/s11528-020-00549-6

Kimmons, R., Graham, C. R., & West, R. E. (2020). The PICRAT model for technology integration in teacher preparation. *Contemporary Issues in Technology and Teacher Education, 20*(1). https://citejournal.org/volume-20/issue-1-20/general/the-picrat-model-for-technology-integration-in-teacher-preparation

Kimmons, R., & Johnstun, K. (2019). Navigating paradigms in educational technology. *TechTrends, 63*, 631–641. https://doi.org/10.1007/s11528-019-00407-0

Kitchen, J. (2005). Conveying respect and empathy: Becoming a relational teacher educator. *Studying Teacher Education, 1*(2), 195–207. https://doi.org/10.1080/17425960500288374

Kitchen, J. (2020). Self-study in teacher education and beyond. In J. Kitchen, A. Berry, S. M. Bullock, A. R. Crowe, M. Taylor, H. Guðjónsdóttir, & L. Thomas (Eds.), *International Handbook of Self-Study of Teaching and Teacher Education Practices* (pp. 1023–1044). Springer. https://doi.org/10.1007/978-981-13-6880-6_34

Klein, M. (2004). The premise and promise of inquiry based mathematics in pre-service teacher education: A poststructuralist analysis. *Asia-Pacific Journal of Teacher Education, 32*(1), 35–47. https://doi.org/10.1080/1359866042000206008

Koehler, M., & Mishra, P. (2009). What is technological pedagogical content knowledge (TPACK)? *Contemporary Issues in Technology and Teacher Education, 9*(1), 60–70.

LaBoskey, V. K. (2004). The methodology of self-study and its theoretical underpinnings. In J. J. Loughran, M. L. Hamilton, V. K. LaBoskey, & T. Russell (Eds.), *International handbook of self-study of teaching and teacher education practices* (Vol. 1, pp. 817–869). Kluwer Academic Publishers.

Lanier, J. E., & Little, J. (1986). Research on teacher education. In M. C. Wittrock (Ed.), *Handbook of research on teaching* (pp. 527–569). Macmillan.

Latchem, C. R., & Robinson, B. (Eds.) (2003), *Teacher education through open and distance learning* (Vol. 3). Psychology Press.

Lave, J., & Wenger, E. (1991). *Situated learning: Legitimate peripheral participation.* Cambridge University Press.

Lay, C. D., Allman, B., Cutri, R. M., & Kimmons, R. (2020). Examining a decade of research in online teacher professional development. *Frontiers in Education, 5*, 167. https://doi.org/10.3389/feduc.2020.573129

Levin, R. A. (1990). Recurring themes and variations. In J. I. Goodlad, R. Soder, & K. A. Sirotnik (Eds.), *Places where teachers are taught* (pp. 40–83). Jossey-Boss.

Loughran, J. (2013). *Developing a pedagogy of teacher education: Understanding teaching & learning about teaching.* Routledge.

134 REFERENCES

Loughran, J., Berry, A., & Mulhall, P. (2012). *Understanding and developing science teachers' pedagogical content knowledge* (Vol. 12). Springer Science & Business Media.

Loughran, J., & Hamilton, M. L. (Eds.). (2016). *International handbook of teacher education.* Springer Science and Business Media.

Martin, A. K. (2017). In search of ways to improve practicum learning: Self-study of the teacher educator/researcher as responsive listener. *Studying Teacher Education, 13*(2), 127–144. https://doi.org/10.1080/17425964.2017.1342347

Masters, J., de Kramer, R. M., O'Dwyer, L., Dash, S., & Russell, M. (2012). The effects of online teacher professional development on fourth grade students' knowledge and practices in English language arts. *Journal of Technology and Teacher Education, 20*(1), 21–46. https://www-learntechlib-org.erl.lib.byu.edu/primary/p/35346/. Accessed on February 12, 2021.

Mayer, D. (2013). The continuing 'problem' of teacher education: Policy driven reforms and the role of teacher educators. In X. Zhu & K. Zeichner (Eds.), *Preparing teachers for the 21st century* (pp. 39–52). Springer. https://doi.org/10.15663/wje.v18i1.133

McMurtrie, B. (2020, March 20). *The coronavirus has pushed courses online: Professors are trying hard to keep up.* The Chronicle of Higher Education. https://www.chronicle.com/article/the-coronavirus-has-pushed-courses-online-professors-are-trying-hard-to-keep-up/. Accessed on February 23, 2021.

McQuiggan, C. A. (2007). The role of faculty development in online teaching's potential to question teaching beliefs and assumptions. *Online Journal of Distance Learning Administration, 10*(3), 1–13.

Miles, M. B., Huberman, A. M., & Saldaña, J. (2018). *Qualitative data analysis: A methods sourcebook.* Sage.

Miller, T., & Ribble, M. (2010). Moving beyond bricks and mortar: Changing the conversation on online education. *Educational Considerations, 37*(2), 3–6. https://www.learntechlib.org/p/107415/. Accessed on February 23, 2021.

Mills, S., Yanes, M., & Casebeer, C. (2009). Perceptions of distance learning among faculty of a college of education. *Journal of Online Learning and Teaching, 5*(1), 19–28. http://jolt.merlot.org/vol5no1/mills_0309.pdf. Accessed on February 23, 2021.

Milman, N. (2020). This is emergency remote teaching, not just online teaching. *Education Week.* https://www.edweek.org/leadership/opinion-this-is-emergency-remote-teaching-not-just-online-teaching/2020/03. Accessed on February 23, 2021.

Mishler, E. (1990). Validation in inquiry-guided research: The role of exemplars in narrative studies. *Harvard Educational Review, 60*(4), 415–443. https://doi.org/10.17763/haer.60.4.n4405243p6635752

Moon, J. A. (1999). *Reflection in learning and professional development: Theory and practice.* Routledge.

Mulvihill, T. M., & Martin, L. E. (2019). Are alternative certification programs necessary?. *The Teacher Educator, 54*(1), 1–3. https://doi.org/10.1080/08878730.2018.1546759

Murphy, M. S., & Pinnegar, S. (2018). Shaping community in online courses: A self-study of practice in course design to support the relational. *Studying Teacher Education, 14*(3), 272–283. https://doi.org/10.1080/17425964.2018.1541236

National Commission on Excellence in Education (NCEE). (1983). A nation at risk: The imperative for educational reform. *The Elementary School Journal, 84*(2), 113–130. https://doi.org/10.1086/461348

National Commission on Teaching and America's Future (NCTAF). (1996). *What matters most: Teaching for America's future (ED573929).* ERIC. https://files.eric.ed.gov/fulltext/ED395931.pdf

National Research Council (NRC). (2010). *Preparing teachers: Building evidence for sound policy.* National Academies Press.

Newberry, M. (2014). Teacher educator identity development of the nontraditional teacher educator. *Studying Teacher Education, 10*(2), 163–178. https://doi.org/10.1080/17425964.2014.903834

Niess, M. L. (2011). Investigating TPACK: Knowledge growth in teaching with technology. *Journal of Educational Computing Research, 44*(3), 299–317. https://doi.org/10.2190%2FEC.44.3.c

References

North American Council for Online Learning (NACOL). (2007). *Research committee issues brief: Professional development for virtual schooling and online learning (ED509632)*. https://files.eric. ed.gov/fulltext/ED509632.pdf

Opfer, V. D., & Pedder, D. (2011). Conceptualizing teacher professional learning. *Review of Educational Research, 81*(3), 376–407. https://doi.org/10.3102%2F0034654311413609

Pantić, N., & Wubbels, T. (2012). Competence-based teacher education: A change from to *Curriculum* culture? *Journal of Curriculum Studies, 44*(1), 61–87. https://doi.org/10.1080/00220272.2011. 620633

Pelliccione, L., Morey, V., & Morrison, C. (2019). An evidence-based case for quality online initial teacher education. *Australasian Journal of Educational Technology, 35*(6), 64–79. https://doi. org/10.14742/ajet.5513

Penuel, W. R., Fishman, B. J., Yamaguchi, R., & Gallagher, L. P. (2007). What makes professional development effective? Strategies that foster curriculum implementation. *American Educational Research Journal, 44*(4), 921–958. https://doi.org/10.3102%2F0002831207308221

Pinnegar, S. (1997). Depending on experience. *Educational Research Quarterly, 21*(2), 43–59.

Pinnegar, S. (2017). Understanding field experiences: The zone of maximal contact and the conundrums and sacred stories in teacher education. *Studying Teacher Education, 13*(2), 210–215. https://doi.org/10.1080/17425964.2017.1342359

Pinnegar, S., & Erickson, L. B. (2009). Uncovering self-studies in teacher education accreditation review processes. In C. A. Lassonde, S. Galman, & C. Kosnik (Eds.), *Self-study research methodologies for teacher educators* (pp. 151–168). Brill. https://doi.org/10.1163/ 9789087906900_010

Pinnegar, S., & Hamilton, M. L. (2009). *Self-study of practice as a genre of qualitative research*. Springer.

Pinnegar, S., & Hamilton, M. L. (Eds.). (2015). *Knowing, becoming, doing as teacher educators: Identity, intimate scholarship, inquiry*. Emerald Publishing Limited.

Pinnegar, S., Hutchinson, D. A., & Hamilton, M. L. (2020). Role of positioning, identity, and stance in becoming S-STTEP researchers. In J. Kitchen, A. Berry, S. M. Bullock, A. R. Crowe, M. Taylor, H. Guðjónsdóttir, & L. Thomas (Eds.), *International handbook of self-study of teaching and teacher education practices* (pp. 97–133). Springer.

Pinnegar, S., Lay, C. D., Andrews, A. B., & Bailey, L. R. (2018). The enduring characteristics of teacher identity: Narratives from teacher leavers In D. Garbet & A. Ovens (Eds.), *Pushing Boundaries and Crossing Borders: Self-study as a Means for Researching Pedagogy* (pp. 481–488). Self-Study of Teacher Education Practices SIG. www.castle-conference.com

Pinnegar, S., Lay, C. D., Bigham, S., & Dulude, C. (2005). Teaching as highlighted by mothering: A narrative inquiry. *Studying Teacher Education, 1*(1), 55–67.

Pinnegar, S. E., Lay, C., Cutri, R. M., & Newberry, M. (2020). Exploring the contribution of self-study of teacher education practice to the conversation on research on teacher education. In C. Edge, A. Cameron-Standerford, & B. Bergh (Eds.), *Textiles and tapestries: Self-study for envisioning new ways of knowing*. EdTech Books. https://edtechbooks.org/textiles_tapestries_self_study/ exploring_contribution

Pinnegar, S., & Murphy, M. S. (2019). Ethical dilemmas of a self-study researcher: A narrative analysis of ethics in the process of S-STEP research. In R. Brandenburg & S. McDonough (Eds.), *Ethics, self-study research methodology, and teacher education* (pp. 117–130). Springer. https:// doi-org.erl.lib.byu.edu/10.1007/978-981-32-9135-5_8

Polanyi, M. (2009). *The tacit dimension*. University of Chicago Press. (Originally published in 1966).

Putnam, H. (2004). *Ethics without ontology*. Harvard University Press.

Redmond, P. (2015). A pedagogical continuum: The journey from face-to-face to online teaching. In P. Redmond, J. Lock, & P. Danaher (Eds.), *Educational innovations and contemporary technologies* (pp. 107–132). Palgrave Macmillan.

Ritchhart, R., Church, M., & Morrison, K. (2011). *Making thinking visible: How to promote engagement, understanding, and independence for all learners*. Jossey-Bass.

Robinson, B., & Latchem, C. R. (2003). Open and distance teacher education: Uses and models. In C. R. Latchem & B. Robinson (Eds.), *Teacher education through open and distance learning* (Vol. 3). Psychology Press.

136 REFERENCES

Rodgers, C. R., & Raider-Roth, M. B. (2006). Presence in teaching. *Teachers and Teaching: Theory and Practice, 12*(3), 265–287. https://doi.org/10.1080/13450600500467548

Saldaña, J. (2016). *The coding manual for qualitative researchers* (3rd ed.). Sage.

Schön, D. A. (1987). *Educating the reflective practitioner: Toward a new design for teaching and learning in the professions.* Jossey-Bass.

Schuck, S., & Russell, T. (2005). Self-study, critical friendship, and the complexities of teacher education. *Studying Teacher Education, 1*(2), 107–121. https://doi.org/10.1080/17425960500288291

Schwab, J. J. (1973). The practical 3: Translation into curriculum. *The School Review, 81*(4), 501–522. https://doi.org/10.1086/443100

Schwab, J. J. (1978). What do scientists do? In I. Westbury & N. J. Wilkof (Eds.), *Science, curriculum, and liberal education: Selected essays* (pp. 184–228). University of Chicago Press. (Original work published 1960)

Schwartz, H. (1996). The changing nature of teacher education. In J. Sikula (Ed.), *Handbook of Research on Teacher Education* (pp. 3–13). Macmillan.

Scott, C., & Dinham, S. (2008). Born not made: The nativist myth and teachers' thinking. *Teacher Development, 12*(2), 115–124. https://doi.org/10.1080/13664530802038105

Sfard, A. (1998). On two metaphors for learning and the dangers of choosing just one. *Educational Researcher, 27*(2), 4–13. https://doi.org/10.3102%2F0013189X027002004

Shulman, L. S. (1986). Those who understand: Knowledge growth in teaching. *Educational Researcher, 15*(4), 4–14.

Sikula, J. (1996). Introduction. In J. Sikula (Ed.), *Handbook of research on teacher education* (pp. xv–xxiii). Macmillan.

Slife, B. D. (2004). Taking practice seriously: Toward a relational ontology. *Journal of Theoretical & Philosophical Psychology, 24*(2), 157–178. https://doi.org/10.1037/h0091239

So, H. J., Lossman, H., Lim, W. Y., & Jacobson, M. J. (2009). Designing an online video based platform for teacher learning in Singapore. *Australasian Journal of Educational Technology, 25*(3). https://doi.org/10.14742/ajet.1144

Sulisworo, D., & Santyasa, I. W. (2018). Maximize the mobile learning interaction through project-based learning activities. *Educational Research and Reviews, 13*(5), 144–149. https://doi.org/10.5897/ERR2018.3463

Thomas, L. (2017). Learning to learn about the practicum: A self-study of learning to support student learning in the field. *Studying Teacher Education, 13*(2), 165–178. https://doi.org/10.1080/17425964.2017.1342354

United Nations Educational, Scientific and Cultural Organization. (2007). *Research analysis: Attracting, developing and retaining effective teachers: A global overview of current policies and practices.* UNESCO. https://unesdoc.unesco.org/ark:/48223/pf0000151685. Accessed on February 23, 2021.

United Nations Educational, Scientific and Cultural Organization. (2020, September 22). COVID-19: How the UNESCO Global Education Coalition is tackling the biggest learning disruption in history https://en.unesco.org/news/civud-19-how-unesco-global-education-coalition-tackling-biggest-learning-disruption-history. Accessed on February 23, 2021.

Van Overschelde, J. P., & Piatt, A. (2020). U.S. Every Student Succeeds Act: Negative impacts on teaching out-of-field. *Research in Educational Policy and Management, 2*(1), 1–22. https://doi.org/10.46303/repam.02.01.1

Vanassche, E., & Berry, A. (2020). Teacher educator knowledge, practice, and S-STTEP research. In J. Kitchen, A. Berry, S. M. Bullock, A. R. Crowe, M. Taylor, H. Guðjónsdóttir, & L. Thomas (Eds.), *International handbook of self-study of teaching and teacher education practices* (pp. 177–213). https://doi.org/10.1007/978-981-13-6880-6_6

Vaughan, N. (2007). Perspectives on blended learning in higher education. *International Journal on E-Learning, 6*(1), 81–94.

Vergroesen, L. L. (2020, July 21). The top challenges for E-learning instructional design in 2020 https://www.eduflow.com/blog/the-top-challenges-for-e-learning-instructional-design-in-2020. Accessed on February 23, 2021.

References

Wambugu, P. W. (2018). Massive Open Online Courses (MOOCs) for professional teacher and teacher educator development: A case of TESSA MOOC in Kenya. *Universal Journal of Educational Research*, *6*(6), 1153–1157.

Wang, Q., & Lu, Z. (2012). A case study of using an online community of practice for teachers' professional development at a secondary school in China. *Learning, Media and Technology*, *37*(4), 429–446. https://doi.org/10.1080/17439884.2012.685077

Whiting, E. F., & Cutri, R. M. (2015). Naming a personal "unearned" privilege: What pre-service teachers identify after a critical multicultural education course. *Multicultural Perspectives*, *17*(1), 13–20. https://doi.org/10.1080/15210960.2014.984717

Wiggins, G. P., & McTighe, J. (2005). *Understanding by design* (2nd ed.). Association for Supervision and Curriculum Development (ASCD).

Yuan, R. (2016). Understanding higher education-based teacher educators' identities in Hong Kong: A sociocultural linguistic perspective. *Asia-Pacific Journal of Teacher Education*, *44*(4), 379–400. https://doi.org/10.1080/1359866X.2015.1094779

Zeichner, K. M. (2010). Rethinking the connections between campus courses and field experiences in college-and university-based teacher education. *Journal of Teacher Education*, *61*(1–2), 89–99. https://doi.org/10.1177%2F0022487109347671

Zeichner, K. M. (2018). *The struggle for the soul of teacher education*. Routledge.

Zeichner, K. M. (2005). A research agenda for teacher education. In M. Cochran-Smith & K. M. Zeichner (Eds.), *Studying teacher education: The report of the AERA Panel on Research and Teacher Education* (pp. 737-759). Lawrence Erlbaum Associates.

Printed and bound by CPI Group (UK) Ltd, Croydon, CR0 4YY
18/12/2024

14614483-0005